THAT OLD-TIME RELIGION

Jordan Maxwell
Paul Tice
and
Alan Snow

with a chapter by Gerald Massey

Published 2000
The Book Tree
Escondido, CA

That Old-Time Religion
ISBN 1-58509-100-6

©2000

THE BOOK TREE

All Rights Reserved

Layout and Design by Tédd St. Rain

Printed on Acid-Free Paper

Published by

The Book Tree
Post Office Box 724
Escondido, CA 92033

We provide fascinating and educational products to help awaken the public to new ideas and information that would not be available otherwise. We carry over 1100 Books, Booklets, Audio, Video, and other products on Alchemy, Alternative Medicine, Ancient America, Ancient Astronauts, Ancient Civilizations, Ancient Mysteries, Ancient Religion and Worship, Angels, Anthropology, Anti-Gravity, Archaeology, Area 51, Assyria, Astrology, Atlantis, Babylonia, Townsend Brown, Christianity, Cold Fusion, Colloidal Silver, Comparative Religions, Crop Circles, The Dead Sea Scrolls, Early History, Electromagnetics, Electro-Gravity, Egypt, Electromagnetic Smog, Michael Faraday, Fatima, The Fed, Fluoride, Free Energy, Freemasonry, Global Manipulation, The Gnostics, God, Gravity, The Great Pyramid, Gyroscopic Anti-Gravity, Healing Electromagnetics, Health Issues, Hinduism, HIV, Human Origins, Jehovah, Jesus, Jordan Maxwell, John Keely, Lemuria, Lost Cities, Lost Continents, Magick, Masonry, Mercury Poisoning, Metaphysics, Mythology, Occultism, Paganism, Pesticide Pollution, Personal Growth, The Philadelphia Experiment, Philosophy, Powerlines, Prophecy, Psychic Research, Pyramids, Rare Books, Religion, Religious Controversy, Roswell, Walter Russell, Scalar Waves, SDI, John Searle, Secret Societies, Sex Worship, Sitchin Studies, Smart Cards, Joseph Smith, Solar Power, Sovereignty, Space Travel, Spirituality, Stonehenge, Sumeria, Sun Myths, Symbolism, Tachyon Fields, Templars, Tesla, Theology, Time Travel, The Treasury, UFOs, Underground Bases, World Control, The World Grid, Zero Point Energy, and much more. Call **1 (800) 700-TREE** for our *FREE BOOK TREECATALOG* or visit our website at www.thebooktree.com for more information.

CONTENTS

UNDERSTANDING WHY THIS BOOK IS IMPORTANT

The Religious traditions of the Western world have origins radically different than we have been taught and the general public believes. The lies and half-truths need to be refuted and Truth brought to light.

Seeking Truth is dangerous work. It helps to have a map — both to know where you are, and where you are going. This book is a map compiled by previous explorers to help you find your way. The authors have traveled different areas of the map, and their views of the landscape may differ, but such is the nature of Truth. The search for Truth leads through many half-truths, dead ends, and false leads, but also leads to great rewards.

Astro-Theology

Gerald Massey's books about the origins of theology were published in the late 1800s until his death in 1907. As an Egyptologist and poet, Massey excelled in getting to the root of assumptions from which a logical arguments develop. His study of Astro-Theology gets to the root orthodox religions assumptions of the Western world.

The Astro-Theology in Massey's study originated in Egypt where similarities to the future Christ figure, of organized and orthodox Christianity, are striking and compelling. It formed the basis of my own study of big religion, big politics, big banking and big business — all too big for their own good, and ours. This article contributed to the opening of my mind. Massey's evidence retains its original power and intellectual honesty.

Stellar Cult

Paul Tice gives a description of the original cult of mankind and how it developed over the generations. Worship of the stars began in Egypt with the worship of Horus, his relatives and colleagues, spreading around the world.

Lunar Cult

Paul Tice brings forward the story of the Stellar Cult into its next incarnation, the Lunar Cult. Man and woman still worship the skies, but incorporate into the rituals the most accessible body in the sky, the moon. While the sun cannot be looked at directly for long without inducing blindness, the moon and its worship can be viewed in its glory occulting and covering the stars as it passes.

Solar Cult

In my contribution I demonstrate the Solar Cult features of what became Christianity, its pagan connections and its roots in astrology. Building on the Stellar Cult and Lunar Cult aspects of the old religion, the Solar Cult superceded them and remains today the religion of the Western world. The pagan connections with the past are shown in the many verses of the Old and New Testaments. Astrology plays a much larger role in Christianity than commonly realized and, in my opinion, forms a basis for much of the doctrines of Christian orthodoxy. I tell the story as I currently understand it, about "That Old-Time Religion."

Dr. Alan Snow on the Dead Sea Scrolls

I interview Dr. Alan Snow on a subject about which he has written extensively — the Dead Sea Scrolls, astrology and the background of Christianity. Dr. Snow's research shows the impact of the Scrolls' discovery on Judaism and Christianity. Dr. Snow explains why the Scrolls were written and the background of the 1st century New Testament world.

The Truth and Mystery of Gnosis

Paul Tice clarifies the role of Gnosticism in its relation to Christianity. Gnosticism was born, grew and flourished as a belief system of personal mysticism mixed with external Christian doctrine during the first four centuries of the Christian era. Gnosis was for the individual, not for the masses.

ASTRO-THEOLOGY
By Gerald Massey

The following article by Gerald Massey will give you a flavor of how I view the subject matter of the origins of religion. It also gives you insight as to how my thought processes work. It provides research material you would never come across in normal reading. This clas-sic article by Gerald Massey was very influential at the turn of the century. I read this article 30 years ago, and was inspired by it. See what you think. —Jordan Maxwell

In presenting my readers with some of the data which show that much of the Christian History was pre-extant as Egyptian mythology, I have to ask you to bear in mind that the facts, like other foundations, have been buried out of sight for thousands of years in a hieroglyphical language, that was never really read by Greek or Roman, and could not be read until the lost clue was discovered by Champollion, almost the other day! In this way the original sources of our Mytholatry and Christology remained as hidden as those of the Nile, until the century in which we live. The mystical matter enshrouded in this language was sacredly entrusted to the keeping of the buried dead, who have faithfully preserved it as their Book of Life, which was placed beneath their pillows, or clasped to their bosoms, in their coffins and their tombs.

Secondly, although I am able to read the hieroglyphics, nothing offered to you is based on my translation. I work too warily for that! The transcription and literal rendering of the hieroglyphic texts herein employed are by scholars of indisputable authority. There is no loophole of escape that way. I lectured upon the subject of Jesus many years ago. At that time I did not know how we had been misled, or that the "Christian scheme" (as it is aptly called) in the New Testament is a fraud, founded on a fable in the Old!

I then accepted the Canonical Gospels as containing a veritable human history, and assumed, as others do, that the history proved itself. Finding that Jesus, or Jehoshua Ben-Pandira, was an historical character, known to the Talmud, I made the common mistake of supposing that this proved the personal existence of the Jesus found portrayed in the Canonical Gospels. But after you have heard my story, and weighed the evidence now for the first time collected and presented to the public, you will not wonder that I should have changed my views, or that I should be impelled to tell the truth to others, as it now appears to myself; although I am only able to summarize here, in the briefest manner possible.

The personal existence of Jesus as Jehoshua Ben-Pandira can be established beyond a doubt. One account affirms that, according to a genuine Jewish tradition, "that man (who is not to be named) was a disciple of Jehoshua Ben-Perachia." It also says, "He was born in the fourth year of the reign of the Jewish King Alexander Jannaeus, notwithstanding the assertions of his followers that he was born in the reign of Herod." That would be more than a century earlier than the date of birth assigned to the Jesus of the Gospels! But it can be further shown that Jehoshua Ben-Pandira may have been born considerably earlier even than the year 102 B.C., although the point is not of much consequence here. Jehoshua, son of Perachia, was a president of the Sanhedrin — the fifth, reckoning from Ezra as the first: one of those who in the line of descent received and transmitted the oral law, as it was said, direct from Sinai. There could not be two of that name. This Ben-Perachia had begun to teach as a Rabbi in the year 104 B.C. We may therefore reckon that he was not born later than 180-170 B.C., and that it could hardly be later than 100 B.C. when he went down into Egypt with his pupil. For it is related that he fled there in consequence of a persecution of the Rabbis, feasibly conjectured to refer to the civil war in which the Pharisees revolted against King Alexander Jannaeus, and consequently about 105 B.C. If we put the age of his pupil, Jehoshua Ben-Pandira, at fifteen years, that will give us an approximate date, extracted without pressure, which shows that Jehoshua Ben-Pandira may have been born about the year 120 B.C. But twenty years are a matter of little moment here.

According to the Babylonian Gemara to the Mishna of Tract "Shabbath," this Jehoshua, the Son of Pandira and Stada, was stoned to death as a wizard, in the city of Lud, or Lydda, and afterwards crucified by being hanged on a tree, on the eve of the Passover. This is the manner of death assigned to Jesus in the Book of Acts. The Gemara says there exists a tradition that on the rest-day before the Sabbath they crucified Jehoshua, on the rest day of the Passah (the day before the Passover). The year of his death, however, is not given in that account; but there are reasons for thinking it could not have been much earlier nor later than B.C. 70, because this Jewish King Janneus reigned from the year 106 to 79 B.C. He was succeeded in the government by his widow Salome, whom the Greeks called Alexandra, and who reigned for some nine years. Now the traditions, especially of the first "Toledoth Jehoshua," relate that the Queen of Jannaeus, and the mother of Hyrcanus, who must therefore be Salome, in spite of her being called by another name, showed favour to Jehoshua and his teaching; that she was a witness to his wonderful works and powers of healing, and tried to save him from the hands of his sacerdotal enemies, because he was related to her; but that during her reign, which ended in the year 71 B.C., he was put to death. The Jewish writers and Rabbis with whom I have talked always deny the identity of the Talmudic Jehoshua and the Jesus of the Gospels. "This," observes Rabbi Jechiels, "which has been related of Jehoshua Ben-Perachia and his pupil, contains no reference whatever to him whom the Christians honour as God!" Another Rabbi, Salman Zevi, produced ten reasons for concluding that Jehoshua of the Talmud was not he who was afterwards called Jesus of Nazareth. Jesus of Nazareth (and of the Canonical Gospels) was unknown to Justus, to the Jew of Celsus, and to Josephus, the supposed references to him by the latter being an undoubted forgery.[1]

---

[1]See Acts 5:30, 10:39, 13:29. More specific is *Sanhedrin 43a* of the Talmud ("Yeshu" is Hebrew for Jesus):

> On the eve of the Passover Yeshu the Nazarean was hanged. For forty days before the execution took place, a herald went forth and cried,
>
>> "He is going forth to be stoned because he has practiced sorcery and enticed Israel to apostacy. Any one who can say anything in his favour, let him come forward and plead on his behalf."
>
> But since nothing was brought forward in his favour *he was hanged* on the eve of Passover.

Emphasis from the above quote is Ernest L. Martin's from his *Secrets of Golgotha: The Forgotten History of Christ's Crucifixion* (Alhambra, CA: Associates for Scriptural Knowledge, 1988), pp. 194–195, showing a viewpoint different from Massey's.

The "blasphemous writings of the Jews about Jesus," as Justin Martyr calls them, always refer to Jehoshua Ben-Pandira, and not to the Jesus of the Gospels. It is Ben-Pandira they mean when they say they have another and a truer account of the birth and life, the wonder-working and death of Jehoshua, or Jesus. This repudiation is perfectly honest and soundly based. The only Jesus known to the Jews was Jehoshua Ben-Pandira, who had learnt the arts of magic in Egypt, and who was put to death by them as a sorcerer. This was likewise the only Jesus known to Celsus, the writer of the "True Logos," a work which the Christians managed to get rid of altogether, with so many other of the anti-Christian evidences.

Celsus observes that he was not a pure Word, not a true Logos, but a man who had learned the arts of sorcery in Egypt. So, in the Clementines, it is in the character of Ben-Pandira that Jesus is said to rise again as the magician. But here is the conclusive fact: The Jews know nothing of Jesus, the Christ of the Gospels, as an historical character; and when the Christians of the fourth century trace his pedigree, by the hand of Epiphanius, they are forced to derive their Jesus from Pandira! Epiphanius gives the genealogy of the Canonical Jesus in this wise:

Jacob, called Pandira, Mary = Joseph — Cleopas, Jesus.

This proves that in the fourth century the pedigree of Jesus was traced to Pandira, the father of that Jehoshua who was the pupil of Ben-Perachia, and who became one of the magicians in Egypt, and who was crucified as a magician on the eve of the Passover by the Jews, in the time of Queen Alexandra, who had ceased to reign in the year 70 B.C. — the Jesus, therefore, who lived and died more than a century too soon.

Thus, the Jews do not identify Jehoshua Ben-Pandira with the Gospel Jesus, of whom they, his supposed contemporaries, know nothing, but protest against the assumption as an impossibility; whereas the Christians do identify their Jesus as the descendent of Pandira. It was he or nobody; yet he was neither the son of Joseph nor the Virgin Mary, nor was he crucified at Jerusalem. It is not the Jews, then, but the Christians, who fuse two supposed historic characters into one! There being but one history acknowledged or known on either side, it follows that the Jesus of the Gospels is the Jehoshua of the Talmud, or is not at all, as a person. This shifts the historical basis altogether; it antedates the human history by more than a hundred years, and it at once destroys the historic character of the Gospels, together with that of any other personal Jesus than Ben-Pandira. In short, the Jewish history of the matter will be found to corroborate the mythical. As Epiphanius knew of no other historical Jesus than the descendant of Pandira, it is possible that this is the Jesus whose tradition is reported by Irenaeus.

Irenaeus was born in the early part of the second century, between 120 and 140 A.D. He was Bishop of Lyons, France, and a personal acquaintance of Polycarp; and he repeats a tradition testified to by the elders, which he alleges was directly derived from John, the "disciple of the Lord," to the effect that Jesus was not crucified at 33 years of age, but that he passed through every age, and lived on to be an oldish man. Now, in accordance with the dates given, Jehoshua Ben-Pandira may have been between 50 and 60 years of age when put to death, and his tradition alone furnishes a clue to the Nihilistic statement of Irenaeus.

When the true tradition of Ben-Pandira is recovered, it shows that he was the sole historical Jesus who was hanged on a tree by the Jews, not crucified in the Roman fashion, and authenticates the claim now to be made on behalf of the astronomical allegory to the dispensational Jesus, the Kronian Christ, the mythical Messiah of the Canonical Gospels, and the Jesus of Paul, who was not the carnalized Christ. For I hold that the Jesus of the "other Gospel" according to the Apostles Cephas and James, who was utterly repudiated by Paul, was none other than Ben-Pandira, the Nazarene, of whom James was a follower, according to a comment on him found in the Book Abodazura. Anyway, there are two Jesuses, or Jesus and the Christ, one of whom is repudiated by Paul.

But Jehoshua, the son of Pandira, can never be converted into Jesus Christ, the son of a virgin mother, as a historic character. Nor can the dates given ever be reconciled with contemporary history. The historical Herod, who sought to slay the young child Jesus, is known to have died four years before the date of the Christian era, assigned for the birth of Jesus.

So much for the historic Jesus. And now for the mythical Christ. Here we can tread on firmer ground.

The mythical Messiah was always born of a Virgin Mother — a factor unknown in natural phenomena, and one that cannot be historical, one that can only be explained by means of the Mythos, and those conditions of primitive sociology which are mirrored in mythology and preserved in the theology. The virgin mother had been represented in Egypt by the maiden Queen, Mut-em-ua, the future mother of Amenhept III, some 16 centuries B.C., who impersonated the eternal virgin that produced the eternal child.

Four consecutive scenes reproduced in my book are found portrayed upon the innermost walls of the *Holy of Holies* in the Temple of Luxor, which was built by Amenhept III, a Pharaoh of the 17th dynasty. The first scene on the left hand shows the God Taht, the Lunar Mercury, the Annunciator of the Gods, in the act of hailing the Virgin Queen, and announcing to her that she is to give birth to the coming Son. In the next scene the God Kneph (in conjunction with Hathor) gives the new life. This is the Holy Ghost or Spirit that causes the Immaculate Conception. Kneph being the spirit by name in Egyptian. The natural effects are made apparent in the virgin's swelling form.

Next the mother is seated on the midwife's stool, and the newborn child is supported in the hands of one of the nurses. The fourth scene is that of the Adoration. Here the child is enthroned, receiving homage to the Gods and gifts from men. Behind the deity of Kneph, on the right, three spirits — the Three Magi, or Kings of the Legend, are kneeling and offering presents with their right hand, and life with their left. The child thus announced, incarnated, born, and worshipped, was the Pharaonic representative of the Aten Sun in Egypt, the God Adon of Syria, and Hebrew Adonai; the child-Christ of the Aten Cult; the miraculous conception of the ever-virgin mother, personated by Mut-em-ua, as mother of the "only one," and representative of the divine mother of the youthful Sun-God.

These scenes, which were mythical in Egypt, have been copied or reproduced as historical in the Canonical Gospels, where they stand like four corner-stones to the Historic Structure, and prove that the foundations are mythical.

Jesus was not only born of the mythical motherhood; his descent on the maternal side is traced in accordance with this origin of the mythical Christ. The virgin was also called the harlot, because she represented the pre-monogamic stage of intercourse; and Jesus descends from four forms of the harlot — Tamar, Rahab, Ruth, and Bathsheba — each of whom is a form of the "stranger in Israel," and is not a Hebrew woman. Such history, however, does not show that illicit intercourse was the natural mode of the divine descent; nor does it imply unparalleled human profligacy. It only proves the Mythos.

In human sociology the son of the mother preceded the father, as son of the woman who was a mother, not a wife. This character is likewise claimed for Jesus, who is made to declare that he was earlier than Abraham, who was the typical Great Father of the Jews; whether considered to be mythical or historical. Jesus states emphatically that he existed before Abraham was. This was only possible to the mythical Christ, who preceded the father as son of the virgin mother; and we shall find it so throughout. All that is non-natural and impossible as human history, is possible, natural and explicable as Mythos.

It can be explained by the Mythos, because it originated in that which alone accounts for it. For it comes to this at last: the more hidden the meaning of the

Gospel history, the more satisfactorily is it explained by the Mythos; and the more mystical the Christian doctrine, the more easily can it be proved to be mythical.

The birth of Christ is astronomical. The birthday is determined by the full moon of Easter. This can only occur once every 19 years, as we have it illustrated by the Epact or Golden Number of the Prayer Book. Understand me! Jesus, the Christ, can only have a birthday, or resurrection, once in 19 years, in accordance with the Metonic Cycle, because his parents are the sun and moon; and those appear in the earliest known representation of the Man upon the Cross! This proves the astronomical and non-human nature of the birth itself, which is identical with that of the full moon of Easter in Egypt.

Cassini, the Italian Astronomer, has demonstrated the fact that the date assigned for the birth of the Christ is an Astronomical epoch in which the middle conjunction of the moon with the sun happened on the 24th March, at half-past one o'clock in the morning, at the meridian of Jerusalem, the very day of the middle equinox. The following day (the 25th) was the day of the Incarnation, according to Augustine, but the date of the Birth, according to Clement Alexander. For two birthdays are assigned to Jesus by the Christian Fathers, one at the Winter Solstice, the other at the Vernal Equinox. These, which cannot both be historical, are based on the two birthdays of the double Horus in Egypt. Plutarch tells us that Isis was delivered of Horus, the child, about the time of the winter Solstice, and that the festival of the second or adult Horus followed the Vernal Equinox. Hence, the Solstice and spring Equinox were both assigned to the one birth of Jesus by the Christolators; and again, that which is impossible as human history is the natural fact in relation to the two Horuses, the dual form of the Solar God in Egypt.

And here, in passing, we may point out the astronomical nature of the Crucifixion. The Gospel according to John brings on a tradition so different from that of the Synoptics as to invalidate the human history of both. The Synoptics say that Jesus was crucified on the 15th of the month Nisan. John affirms that it was on the 14th of the month. This serious rift runs through the very foundation! As human history it cannot be explained. But there is an explanation possible, which, if accepted, proves the Mythos. The Crucifixion (or Crossing) was, and still is, determined by the full moon of Easter. This, in the lunar reckoning, would be on the 14th in a month of 28 days; in the solar month of 30 days it was reckoned to occur on the 15th of the month. Both unite, and the rift closes in proving the Crucifixion to have been Astronomical, just as it was in Egypt, where the two dates can be identified.

Plutarch also tells us how the Mithraic Cult had been particularly established in Rome about the year 70 B.C. And Mithras was fabled as having been born in a cave. Wherever Mithras was worshipped the cave was consecrated as his birthplace. The cave can be identified, and the birth of the Messiah in that cave, no matter under what name he was born, can be definitely dated. The "Cave of Mithras" was the birthplace of the Sun in the Winter Solstice, when this occurred on the 25th of December in the sign of the Sea-Goat, with the Vernal Equinox in the sign of the Ram. Now the Akkadian name of the tenth month, that of the Sea-Goat, which answers roughly to our December, the tenth by name, is *Abba Uddu*, that is, the "Cave of Light"; the cave of re-birth for the Sun in the lowest depth of the Solstice, figured as the Cave of Light. This cave was continued as the birthplace of the Christ. You will find it in all the Gospels of the Infancy, and Justin Martyr says, "Christ was born in the Stable, and afterwards took refuge in the Cave." He likewise vouches for the fact that Christ was born on the same day that the Sun was re-born in *Stabulo Augioe*, or, in the Stable of Augias. Now the cleansing of this Stable was the sixth Labor of Hercules, his first being in the sign of the Lion; and Justin was right; the Stable and Cave are both figured in the same Celestial Sign. But mark this! the Cave was the birthplace of the Solar Messiah from the year 2410 to the year 255 B.C., at which latter date the Solstice passed out of the Sea-Goat into the sign of the Archer; and no Messiah, whether called Mithras, Adon, Tammuz, Horus or Christ, could have been born in the Cave of *Abba Uddu* or the Stable of Augias on the 25th of December after the year 255 B.C.; therefore, Justin had nothing but the Mithraic tradition of the by-gone birthday to prove the birth of the Historical Christ 255 years later!

In their mysteries the Sarraceni celebrated the Birth of the babe in the Cave or Subterranean Sanctuary, from which the Priest issued, and cried: — "The Virgin hath brought forth: The Light is about to begin to grow again!" — on the Mother-night of the year. And the Sarraceni were *not* supporters of Historic Christianity.

The birthplace of the Egyptian Messiah at the Vernal Equinox was figured in Apt, or Apta, the corner; but Apta is also the name of the Crib and the Manger; hence the Child born in Apta was said to be born in a manger; and this Apta as Crib or Manger is the hieroglyphic sign of the Solar birthplace. Hence the Egyptians exhibited the Babe in the Crib or Manger in the streets of Alexandria. The birth-place was indicated by the colure of the Equinox, as it passed from sign to sign. It was also pointed out by the Star in the East. When the birthplace was in the sign of the Bull, Orion was the Star that rose in the East to tell where the young Sun-God was re-born. Hence it is called the "Star of Horus." That was then the Star of the "Three Kings" who greeted the Babe; for the "Three Kings" is still a name of the three stars in Orion's Belt. Here we learn that the legend of the "Three Kings" is at least 6,000 years old.

In the course of Precession, about 255 B.C., the vernal birthplace passed into the sign of the fishes, and the Messiah who had been represented for 2155 years by the Ram or Lamb, and previously for other 2155 years by the Apis Bull, was now imaged as the Fish, or the "Fish-man," called Ichthys in Greek. The original Fish-man — the An of Egypt, and the Oan of Chaldea — probably dates from the pre-vious cycle of precession, or 26,000 years earlier; and about 255 B.C. the Messiah, as the Fish-man, was to come up once more as the Manifestor from the celestial waters. The coming Messiah is called Dag, the Fish, in the Talmud; and the Jews at one time connected his coming with some conjunction, or occurrence, in the sign of the Fishes! This shows the Jews were not only in possession of the astronomical allegory, but also of the tradition by which it could be interpreted. It was the Mythical and Kronian Messiah alone who was, or could be, the subject of prophe-cy that might be fulfilled — prophecy that was fulfilled as it is in the Book of Revelation — when the Equinox entered, the cross was re-erected, and the founda-tions of a new heaven were laid in the sign of the Ram, 2410 B.C.; and, again, when the Equinox entered the sign of the Fishes, 255 B.C. Prophecy that will be *again* fulfilled when the Equinox enters the sign of the Waterman about the end of this [the 19th] century, to which the Samaritans are still looking forward for the com-ing of their Messiah, who has not yet arrived for them. The Christians alone ate the oyster; the Jews and Samaritans only got an equal share of the empty shells! The uninstructed Jews, the *idiotai*, at one time thought the prophecy which was astro-nomical and solely related to the cycles of time, was to have its fulfillment in human history. But they found out their error, and bequeathed it unexplained to the still more ignorant Christians. The same tradition of the Coming One is extant amongst the Millenarians and Adventists, as amongst the Moslems. It is the tradi-tion of El-Mahdi, the prophet who is to come in the last days of the world to con-quer all the world, and who was lately descending the Sudan with the old announcement "Day of the Lord is at hand," which shows that the astronomical allegory has left some relics of the true tradition among the Arabs, who were at one time learned in astronomical lore.

The Messiah, as the Fish-man, is foreseen by Esdras ascending out of the sea as the "same whom God the highest hath kept a great season, which by his own self shall deliver the creature." The ancient Fish-man only came up out of the sea to converse with men and teach them in the daytime. "When the sun set," says

Berosus, "it was the custom of this Being to plunge again into the sea, and abide all night in the deep." So the man foreseen by Esdras is only visible by day.

As it is said, "E'en so can no man upon earth see my son, or those that be with him, but in the daytime." This is parodied or fulfilled in the account of Ichthys, the Fish, the Christ who instructs men by day, but retires to the lake of Galilee, where he demonstrates his solar nature by walking the waters at night, or at the dawn of day.

We are told that his disciples being on board a ship, "when even was come, in the fourth watch of the night, Jesus went unto them walking upon the sea." Now the fourth watch began at three o'clock, and ended at six o'clock. Therefore, this was about the proper time for a solar God to appear walking upon the waters, or coming up out of them as the Oannes. Oannes is said to have taken no food whilst he was with men: "In the daytime he used to converse with men, but took no food at that season." So Jesus, when his disciples prayed him, saying "Master, eat," said unto them, "I have meat to eat that you know not of. My meat is to do the will of Him that sent me."

This is the perfect likeness of the character of Oannes, who took no food, but whose time was wholly spent in teaching men. Moreover, the mythical Fish-man is made to identify himself. When the Pharisees sought a "sign from heaven," Jesus said, "There shall no sign be given but the sign of Jonas. For as Jonas became a sign unto the Ninevites, so shall also the son of man be to this generation."

The sign of Jonas is that of the Oan, or Fish-man of Nineveh, whether we take it direct from the monuments, or from the Hebrew history of Jonah, or from the Zodiac.

The voice of the secret wisdom here says truly that those who are looking for signs, can have no other than that of the returning Fish-man, Ichthys, Oannes, or Jonah; and assuredly, there was no other sign or date — than those of Ichthys, the Fish who was re-born of the fish-goddess, Atergatis, in the sign of the Fishes, 255 B.C., after whom the primitive Christians were called little fishes, or Piscuculi.

This date of 255 B.C. was the true day of birth, or rather of re-birth for the celestial Christ, and there was no valid reason for changing the time of the world.

The Gospels contain a confused and confusing record of early Christian belief: things most truly believed (Luke) concerning certain mythical matters, which were ignorantly mistaken for human and historical. The Jesus of our Gospels is but little of a human reality, in spite of all attempts to naturalize the Mythical Christ, and make the story look rational.

The Christian religion was not founded on a man, but on a divinity; that is, a mythical character. So far from being derived from the model man, the typical Christ was made up from the features of various Gods, after a fashion somewhat like those "pictorial averages" portrayed by Mr. Galton, in which the traits of several persons are photographed and fused in a portrait of a dozen different persons, merged into one that is not anybody. And as fast as the composite Christ falls to pieces, each feature is claimed, each character is gathered up by the original owner, as with the grasp of gravitation.

It is not that I deny the divinity of Jesus the Christ; I assert it! He never was, and never could be, any other than a divinity; that is, a character non-human, and entirely mythical, who had been the pagan divinity of various pagan myths, that had been pagan during thousands of years before our Era.

Nothing is more certain, according to honest evidence, than that the Christian scheme of redemption is founded on a fable misinterpreted; that the prophecy of fulfillment was solely astronomical, and the Coming One as the Christ who came in the end of an age, or of the world, was but a metaphorical figure, a type of time, from the first, which never could take form in historic personality, any more than

Time in Person could come out of a clock-case when the hour strikes; that no Jesus could become a Nazarene by being born at, or taken to, Nazareth; and that the history in our Gospels is from beginning to end the identifiable story of the Sun-God, and the Gnostic Christ who never could be made flesh. When we did not know the one it was possible to believe the other; but when once we truly know, then the false belief is no longer possible.

The mythical Messiah was Horus in the Osirian Mythos; Har-Khuti in the Sut-Typhonian; Khunsu in that of Amen-Ra; Iu in the cult of Atum-Ra; and the Christ of the Gospels is an amalgam of all these characters.

The Christ is the Good Shepherd!

So was Horus

Christ is the Lamb of God!

So was Horus

Christ is the Bread of Life!

So was Horus

Christ is the Truth and the Life!

So was Horus

Christ is the Fan-bearer!

So was Horus

Christ is the Lord!

So was Horus

Christ is the Way and the Door of Life!

Horus was the path in which they traveled out of the Sepulchre. He is the God whose name is written with the hieroglyphic sign of the Road or Way.

Jesus is he that should come; and Iu, the root of the name in Egyptian, means "to come." Iu-em-hept, as the Su, the Son of Atum, or of Ptah, was the "Ever-Coming One," who is always portrayed as the marching youngster, in the act and attitude of coming. Horus included both sexes;. The Child (or the soul) is of either sex, and potentially, of both. Hence the hermaphrodital Deity; and Jesus, in Revelation, is the Young Man who was the female paps.

Iu-em-hept signifies him who comes with peace. This is the character in which Jesus is announced by the Angels! And when Jesus comes to his disciples after the resurrection it is as the bringer of peace. "Learn of me and ye shall find rest," says the Christ. Khunsu-Nefer-Hept is the Good Rest, Peace in Person! The Egyptian Jesus, Iu-em-hept, was the second Atum; Paul's Jesus is the second Adam. In one rendition of John's Gospel, instead of the "only-begotten Son of God," a variant reading gives the "only-begotten God," which has been declared an impossible rendering. But the "only-begotten God," was an especial type in the Egyptian Mythology, and the phrase re-identifies the divinity whose emblem is the beetle. Hor-Apollo says, "To denote the only-begotten or a father, the Egyptians delineate a scarabaeus! By this they symbolize an only-begotten, because the creature is self-produced, being unconceived by a female." Now the youthful manifestor of the Beetle-God was this Iu-em-hept, the Egyptian Jesus. The very phraseology of John is common to the Inscriptions, which tell of him who was the beginner of Becoming from the first, and who made all things, but who himself was not made. I quote verbatim, and not only was the Beetle-God continued in the "only-begotten God"; the beetle-type was also brought on as a symbol of the Christ. Ambrose and Augustine, among the Christian Fathers, identified Jesus with, and as, the "good Scarabaeus," which further identifies the Jesus of John's Gospel with the Jesus of Egypt, who was the Ever-Coming One, and the Bringer of Peace, whom I have elsewhere shown to be the Jesus to whom the Book of Ecclesiasticus is inscribed, and ascribed in the Apocrypha.

In accordance with this continuation of the Kamite symbols, it was also maintained by some sectaries that Jesus was a potter, and not a carpenter; and the fact is that this only-begotten Beetle-God, who is portrayed sitting at the potter's wheel forming the Egg, or shaping the vase-symbol of creation, was the Potter personified, as well as the only-begotten God in Egypt.

The character and teachings of the Canonical Christ are composed of contradictions which cannot be harmonized as those of a human being, whereas they are always true to the Mythos.

He is the Prince of Peace, and yet he asserts that he came not to bring peace: "I came not to send peace, but a sword," and not only is Iu-em-hept the Bringer of Peace by name in one character; he is the Sword personified in the other. In this he says, "I am the living image of Atum, proceeding from him as a sword." Both characters belong to the mythical Messiah in the Ritual, who also calls himself the "Great Disturber," and the "Great Tranquilizer" — the "God Contention," and "God Peace." The Christ of the Canonical Gospels has several prototypes, and sometimes the copy is derived or the trait is caught from one original, and sometimes from the other. The Christ of Luke's Gospel has a character entirely distinct from that of John's Gospel. Here he is the Great Exorciser, and caster-out of demons. John's Gospel contains no case of possession or obsession: no certain man who "had devils this long time"; no child possessed with a devil; no blind and dumb man possessed with a devil.

Other miracles are performed by the Christ of John, but not these; because John's is a different type of Christ. And the original of the Great Healer in Luke's Gospel may be found in the God Khunsu, who was the Divine Healer, the supreme one amongst all the other healers and saviours, especially as the caster-out of demons, and the expeller of possessing spirits. He is called in the texts the "Great God, the driver away of possession."

In the Stele of the "Possessed Princess," this God in his effigy is sent for by the chief of Bakhten, that he may come and cast out a possessing spirit from the king's daughter, who has an evil movement in her limbs. The demon recognizes the divinity just as the devil recognizes Jesus, the expeller of evil spirits. Also the God Khunsu is Lord over the pig — a type of Typhon. He is portrayed in the disk of the full moon of Easter, in the act of offering the pig as a sacrifice. Moreover, in the judgment scenes, when the wicked spirits are condemned and sent back into the abyss, their mode of return to the lake of primordial matter is by entering the bodies of swine. Says Horus to the Gods, speaking of the condemned one: "When I sent him to his place he went, and he has been transformed into a black pig." So when the Exorcist in Luke's Gospel casts out Legion, the devils ask permission of the Lord of the pig to be allowed to enter the swine, and he gives them leave. This, and much more that might be adduced, tends to differentiate the Christ of Luke, and to identify him with Khunsu, rather than with Iu-em-hept, the Egyptian Jesus, who is reproduced in the Gospel according to John. In this way it can be proved that the history of Christ in the Gospels is one long and complete catalogue of likenesses to the Mythical Messiah, the Solar or Luni-Solar God.

The "Litany of Ra," for example, is addressed to the Sun-God in a variety of characters, many of which are assigned to the Christ of the Gospels. Ra is the Supreme Power, the Beetle that rests in the Empyrean, who is born as his own son. This, as already said, is the God in John's Gospel, who says: — "I and the Father are one," and who is the father born as his own son; for he says, in knowing and seeing the son, "from henceforth ye know him and have seen him", i.e. the Father.

Ra is designated the "Soul that speaks." Christ is the Word. Ra is the destroyer of venom. Jesus says: — "In my name they shall take up serpents, and if they drink any deadly thing it shall not hurt them." In one character Ra is the outcast. So Jesus had not where to lay his head.

Ra is the "timid one who sheds tears in the form of the Afflicted." He is called Remi, the Weeper. This weeping God passes through "Rem-Rem," the place of weeping, and there conquers on behalf of his followers. In the Ritual the God says: — "I have desolated the place of Rem-Rem." This character is sustained by Jesus in the mourning over Jerusalem that was to be desolated. The words of John, "Jesus wept," are like a carven statue of the "Afflicted One," as Remi, the Weeper. Ra is also the God who "makes the mummy come forth." Jesus makes the mummy come forth in the shape of Lazarus; and in the Roman Catacombs the risen Lazarus is not only represented as a mummy, but is an Egyptian mummy which has been eviscerated and swathed for the eternal abode. Ra says to the mummy: "Come forth!" and Jesus cries: "Lazarus, come forth!" Ra manifests as "the burning one, he who sends destruction," or "sends his fire into the place of destruction." "He sends fire upon the rebels," his form is that of the "god of the furnace." Christ also comes in the person of this "burning one"; the sender of destruction by fire. He is proclaimed by Matthew to be the Baptizer with fire. He says, "I am come to send fire on the earth."

He is portrayed as "God of the furnace," which shall "burn up the chaff with unquenchable fire." He is to cast the rebellious into a "furnace of fire," and send the condemned ones into everlasting fire. All this was natural when applied to the Solar-God, and it is supposed to become supernatural when misapplied to a supposed human being to whom it never could apply. The Solar fire was the primary African found of the theological hell-fire and hell.

The "Litany" of Ra collects the manifold characters that make up the total God (termed Teb-temt), and the Gospels have gathered up the mythical remains; thus the result is in each case identical, or entirely similar. From beginning to end the Canonical Gospels contain the Drama of the Mysteries of the Luni-Solar God, narrated as a human history. The scene on the Mount of Transfiguration is obviously derived from the ascent of Osiris into the Mount of Transfiguration in the Moon. The sixth day was celebrated as that of the change and transformation of the Solar God in the lunar orb, which he re-entered on that day as the regenerator of its light. With this we may compare the statement made by Matthew, that "after six days Jesus went up into a high mountain apart, and he was transfigured, and his face did shine as the sun (of course!), and his garments became white as the light."

In Egypt the year began just at the Summer Solstice, when the sun descended from its midsummer height lost its force, and lessened in its size. This represented Osiris, who was born of the Virgin Mother as the child Horus, the diminished infantile sun of Autumn; the suffering, wounded, bleeding Messiah, as he was represented. He descended into hell, or hades, where he was transformed into the virile Horus, and rose again as the sun of the resurrection at Easter. In these two characters of Horus on the two horizons, Osiris furnished the dual type of the Canonical Christ, which shows very satisfactorily how the mythical prescribes the boundaries beyond which the historical does not, dare not, go. The first was the child Horus, who always remained a child. In Egypt the boy or girl wore the Horus look of childhood until 12 years of age. Thus childhood ended about the twelfth year. But although adultship was then entered upon by the youth, and the transformation of the boy into manhood began, the full adultship was not attained until 30 years of age. The man of 30 years was the typical adult. The age of adultship was 30 years, as it was in Rome under the *Lex Pappia*. The *homme fait* is the man whose years are triaded by tens, and who is *Khemt*. As with the man, so it is with the God; and the second Horus, the same God is his second character, is the *Khemt* or *Khem-Horus*, the typical adult of 30 years. The God who gave up twelve years was Horus, the child of Isis, the mother's child, the weakling. The virile Horus (the sun in its vernal strength), the adult of 30 years, was representative of the Fatherhood, and this Horus is the anointed son of Osiris. These two characters of Horus the child, and Horus the adult of 30 years, are reproduced in the only two phases of Jesus'life in the Gospels. John furnishes no historic dates for the time when the *Word* was incarnated and became flesh; nor for the childhood of Jesus; nor for the tra[n]s-mation into the Messiah. But Luke tells us that *the child of twelve years* was [a] wonderful youth, and that he increased in wisdom and stature. This is the length [of] years assigned to Horus the child; and this phase of the child-Christ's life is fol-lowed by the baptism and anointing, the descent of the pubescent spirit with the consecration of the Messiah in Jordan, when Jesus "began to be about 30 years of age."

The earliest anointing was the consecration of puberty; and here at the full age of the typical adult, the Christ, who was previously a child, the child of the Virgin Mother, is suddenly made into the Messiah, as the Lord's anointed. And just as the second Horus was regenerated, and this time begotten of the father, so in the trans-formation scene of the baptism in Jordan, the father authenticates the change into full adultship, with the voice from heaven saying: — "This is my beloved son, in whom I am well pleased;" the spirit of pubescence, or the *Ruach*, being represent-ed by the descending dove, called the spirit of God. Thus from the time when the child-Christ was about twelve years of age, until that of the typical *homme fait* of Egypt, which was the age assigned to Horus when he became the adult God, there is no history. This is in exact accordance with the Kamite allegory of the double-Horus. And the Mythos alone will account for the chasm which is wide and deep enough to engulf a supposed history of 18 years. Childhood cannot be carried beyond the 12th year, and the child Horus always remained a child; just as the child-Christ does in Italy, and in German folk-tales. The mythical record founded on nature went no further, and there the history consequently halts within the pre-scribed limits, to rebegin with the anointed and regenerated Christ at the age of Khem-Horus, the adult of 30 years.

And these two characters of Horus necessitated a double form of the mother, who divides into the two divine sisters, Isis and Nephthys. Jesus also was by-mater, or dual-mothered; and the two sisters reappear in the Gospels as the two Marys, both of whom are the mothers of Jesus. This again, which is impossible as human history, is perfect according to the Mythos that explains it.

As the child-Horus, Osiris comes down to earth; he enters matter, and becomes mortal. He is born like the Logos, or "as a Word." His father is Seb, the earth, whose consort is Nu, the heaven, one of whose names is Meri, the Lady of Heaven; and these two are the prototypes of Joseph and Mary. He is said to cross the earth as a substitute, and to suffer vicariously as the Savior, Redeemer, and Justifier of man. In these two characters there was constant conflict between Osiris and Typhon, the Evil Power, or Horus and Sut, the Egyptian Satan. At the Autumn Equinox, the devil of darkness began to dominate; this was the Egyptian Judas, who betrayed Osiris to his death at the last supper. On the day of the Great Battle at the Vernal Equinox, Osiris conquered as the ascending God, the Lord of the growing light. Both these struggles are portrayed in the Gospels. In the one Jesus is betrayed to his death by Judas; in the other he rises superior to Satan. The latter conflict fol-lowed immediately after the baptism. In this way: — When the sun was half-way round, from the Lion sign, it crossed the River of the Waterman, the Egyptian Iarutana, Hebrew Jordan, Greek Eridanus. In this water the baptism occurred, and the transformation of the child-Horus into the virile adult, the conqueror of the evil power, took place. Horus becomes hawk-headed, just where the dove descended and abode on Jesus. Both birds represented the virile soul that constituted the anointed one at puberty. By this added power Horus vanquished Sut, and Jesus overcame Satan. Both the baptism and the contest are referred to in the Ritual. "I am washed with the same water in which the Good Opener (Un-Nefer) washes when he disputes with Satan, that justification should be made to Un-Nefer, the Word made Truth," or the Word that is Law.

The scene between the Christ and the Woman at the Well may likewise be found in the Ritual. Here the woman is the lady with the long hair, that is Nu, the

— and the five husbands can be paralleled by her five star-gods born
rinks out of the well "to take away his thirst." He also says: "I am
er. I make way in the valley, in the Pool of the Great One. Make-
ker) expresses what I am." "I am the Path by which they traverse
re of Osiris."

messiah reveals himself as the source of living water, "that springeth up
into Everlasting Life." Later on he says, "I am the way, the truth, the life." "I am
creating the water, discriminating the seat," says Horus. Jesus says, "The hour
cometh when ye shall neither in this mountain nor yet at Jerusalem worship the
Father." Jesus claims that this well of life was given to him by the Father. In the
Ritual it says, "He is thine, O Osiris! A well, or flow, comes out of thy mouth to
him!" Also the paternal source is acknowledged in another text. "I am the Father,
inundating when there is thirst, guarding the water. Behold me at it." Moreover, in
another chapter the well of living water becomes the Pool of Peace. The speaker
says, "The well has come through me. I wash in the Pool of Peace."

In Hebrew, the Pool of Peace is the Pool of Salem, or Siloam. And here, not
only is the pool described at which the Osirified are made pure and healed; not only
does the angel or God descend to the waters — the "certain times" are actually
dated. "The gods of the pure waters are there on the fourth hour of the night, and
the eighth hour of the day, saying, 'Pass away hence,'to him who has been cured."

In the margin, the Pool of Siloam is said to be the Pool of "Sent," and the word
"Sennt" is an Egyptian name for a medicated or healing bath!

An epitome of a considerable portion of John's Gospel may be found in another brief chapter of the Ritual — "Ye Gods come to be my servants, I am the son of
your Lord. Ye are mine through my Father, who gave you to me. I have been among
the servants of Hathor or Meri. I have been washed by thee, O attendant!" Compare
the washing of Jesus' feet by Mary.

The Osiris exclaims, "I have welcomed the chief spirits in the service of the
Lord of things! I am the Lord of the fields when they are white," i.e., for the reapers
and the harvest. So the Christ now says to the disciples, "Behold, I say to you, Lift
up your eyes and look on the fields, that are white already unto the harvest."

"Then said he unto his disciples, 'The harvest truly is plenteous, but the laborers are few. Pray ye, therefore, the Lord of the harvest that he send forth laborers
into his harvest.'And he called unto him his twelve disciples." Now, if we turn to
the Egyptian "Book of Hades," the harvest, the Lord of the harvest, and the reapers
of the harvest are all portrayed: the twelve are also there. In one scene they are preceded by a God leaning on a staff, who is designated the Master of Joy — a sur-
name of the Messiah Horus when assimilated to the Soli-Lunar Khunsu; the twelve
are "they who labor at the harvest in the plains of Neter-Kar." A bearer of a sickle
shows the inscription: "These are the Reapers." The twelve are divided into two
groups of five and seven — the original seven of the Aahenru; these seven are the
reapers. The other five are bending towards an enormous ear of corn, the image of
the harvest, ripe and ready for the sickles of the seven. The total twelve are called
the "Happy Ones," the bearers of food. Another title of the twelve is that of the
"Just Ones." The God says to the reapers, "Take your sickles! Reap your grain!
Honour to you reapers." Offerings are made to them on earth, as bearers of sickles
in the fields of Hades. On the other hand, the tares or the wicked are to be cast out
and destroyed forever. These twelve are the apostles in their Egyptian phase.

In the chapters on "Celestial Diet" in the Ritual, Osiris eats under a sycamore
tree of Hathor. He says, "Let him come from the earth. Thou hast brought these
seven loaves for me to live by, bringing the bread that Horus (the Christ) makes.
Thou hast placed, thou hast eaten rations. Let him call to the Gods for them, or the
Gods come with them to him."

This is reproduced as miracle in the Gospels, performed when the multitude were fed upon seven loaves. The seven loaves are found here, together with the calling upon the gods, or working the miracle of multiplying the bread.

In the next chapter there is a scene of eating and drinking. The speaker, who impersonates the Lord, says: — "I am the Lord of Bread in Annu. My bread at the heaven was that of Ra; my bread on earth was that of Seb." The seven loaves represent the bread of Ra. Elsewhere the number prescribed to be set on one table, as an offering, is five loaves. These are also carried on the heads of five different persons in the scenes of the under-world. Five loaves are the bread of Seb. Thus five loaves represent the bread of earth, and seven the bread of heaven. Both five and seven are sacred regulation numbers in the Egyptian Ritual. And in the Gospel of Matthew the miracles are wrought with five loaves in the one case, and seven in the other, when the multitudes are fed on celestial diet. This will explain the two different numbers in one and the same Gospel miracle. In the Canonical narrative there is a lad with five barley loaves and two fishes. In the next chapter of the Ritual we possibly meet with the lad himself, as the miracle-worker says: — "I have given breath to the said youth."

The Gnostics asserted truly that celestial persons and celestial scenes had been transferred to earth in our Gospels; and it is only within the Pleroma (the heaven) or in the Zodiac that we can at times identify the originals of both. And it is there we must look for the "two fishes."

As the latest form of the Manifestor was in the heaven of the twelve signs, that probably determined the number of twelve basketsful of food remaining when the multitude had all been fed. "They that ate the loaves were five thousand men;" and five thousand was the exact number of the Celestials or Gods in the Assyrian Paradise, before the revolt and fall from heaven. The scene of the miracle of the loaves and fishes is followed by an attempt to take Jesus by force, but he withdrew himself; and this is succeeded by the miracle of his walking on the waters, and conquering the wind and waves. So is it in the Ritual. Chapter 57 is that of the breath prevailing over the water in Hades. The speaker, having to cross over, says: "O Hapi! let the Osiris prevail over the waters, like as the Osiris prevailed against the taking by stealth, the night of the great struggle." The Solar God was betrayed to his death by the Egyptian Judas, on the "night of the taking by stealth," which was the night of the last supper. The God is "waylaid by the conspirators, who have watched very much." They are said to smell him out "by the eating of his bread." So the Christ is waylaid by Judas, who "knew the place, for Jesus often resorted thither," and by the Jews who had long watched to take him.

The smelling of Osiris by the eating of his bread is remarkably rendered by John at the eating of the last supper. The Ritual has it: — "They smell Osiris by the eating of his bread, transporting the evil of Osiris."

"And when he had dipped the sop he gave it to Judas Iscariot, and after the sop Satan entered into him." Then said Jesus to him into whom the evil or devil had been transported, "That thou doest, do quickly." Osiris was the same, beseeching burial. Here it is demonstrable that the non-historical Herod is a form of the Apophis Serpent, called the enemy of the Sun. In Syriac, Herod is a red dragon. Herod, in Hebrew, signifies a terror. Heru (Eg.) is to terrify, and Herrut (Eg.) is the Snake, the typical reptile. The blood of the divine victim that is poured forth by the Apophis Serpent at the sixth hour, on "the night of smiting the profane," is literally shed by Herod, as the Herrut or Typhonian Serpent.

The speaker, in the Ritual, asks: "Who art thou then, Lord of the Silent Body? I have come to see him who is in the serpent, eye to eye, and face to face." "Lord of the Silent Body" is a title of the Osiris. "Who art thou then, Lord of the Silent Body?" is asked and left unanswered. This character is also assigned to the Christ. The High Priest said unto him, "Answerest thou nothing?" "But Jesus held his peace." Herod questioned him in many words, but he answered him nothing. He acts the prescribed character of "Lord of the Silent Body."

The transaction in the sixth hour of the night of the Crucifixion is expressly inexplicable. In the Gospel we read: — "Now from the sixth hour there was darkness over all the land until the ninth hour." The sixth hour being midnight, that shows the solar nature of the mystery, which has been transferred to the sixth hour of the day in the Gospel.

It is in the seventh hour that the moral struggle takes place between the Osiris and the deadly Apophis, or the great serpent, Haber, 450 cubits long, that fills the whole heaven with its vast enveloping folds. The name of this seventh hour is "that which wounds the serpent Haber." In this conflict with the evil power thus portrayed, the Sun-God is designated the "Conqueror of the Grave," and is said to make his advance through the influence of Isis, who aids him in repelling the serpent or devil of darkness. In the Gospel, Christ is likewise set forth in the supreme struggle as "Conqueror of the Grave," for "the graves were opened, and many bodies of the saints which slept arose;" and Mary represents Isis, the mother, at the cross. It is said of the great serpent, "There are those on earth who do not drink of the waters of this serpent, Haber," which may be paralleled with the refusal of the Christ to drink of the vinegar mingled with gall.

When the God has overcome the Apophis Serpent, his old nightly, annual, and eternal enemy, he exclaims,

> I come! I have made my way! I have come like the sun, through the
> gate of the one who likes to deceive and destroy otherwise called the
> 'viper.' I have made my way! I have bruised the serpent, I have
> passed.

But the more express representation in the mysteries was that of the annual sun as the Elder Horus, or Atum. As Julius Firmicus says: "In the solemn celebration of the mysteries, all things in order had to be done which the youth either did or suffered in his death."

Diodorus Siculus rightly identified the "whole fable of the underworld," that was dramatized in Greece, as having been copied "from the ceremonies of the Egyptian funerals," and so brought on from Egypt into Greece and Rome. One part of this mystery was the portrayal of the suffering Sun-God in a feminine phase. When the suffering sun was ailing and ill, he became female, such being a primitive mode of expression. Luke describes the Lord in the Garden of Gethsemane as being in a great agony, "and his sweat was, as it were, great drops of blood, falling to the ground." This experience the Gnostics identified with the suffering of their own hemorrhoidal Sophia, whose passion is the original of that which is celebrated during Passion week, the "week of weeping in Abtu," and which constitutes the fundamental mystery of the rosy Cross, and the Rose of Silence.

In this agony and bloody sweat the Christ simply fulfills the character of Osiris. Tesh-Tesh, the red sun, the Sun-God that suffers his agony means the bleeding, red, gory, separate, cut, and wounded; tesh-tesh is the inert form of the God whose suffering, like that of Adonis, was represented as feminine, which alone reaches a natural origin for the type. He was also called Ans-Ra, or the sun bound up in linen.

So natural were the primitive mysteries!

My attention has just been called to a passage in Lycophron, who lived under Ptolemy Philadelphus between 310 and 246 B.C. In this Hercules is referred to as

> "That three-nighted lion, whom of old
> Triton's fierce dog with furious jaws devoured,
> Within whose bowels, tearing of his liver,
> He rolled, burning with heat, though without fire,
> His head with drops of sweat bedewed all o'er."

This describes the God suffering his agony and sweat, which is called the "bloody flux" of Osiris. Here the nights are three in number. So the Son of Man was to be three nights as well as three days in the "heart of the earth." In the Gospels this prophecy is not fulfilled; but if we include the night of bloody sweat, we have the necessary three nights, and the Mythos becomes perfect. In this phase the suffering Sun was the Red Sun, whence the typical Red Lion.

As Atum, the red sun is described as setting from the Land of Life in all the colors of crimson, or Pant, the red pool. This clothing of colors is represented as a "gorgeous robe" by Luke; a purple robe by Mark; and a robe of scarlet by Matthew. As he goes down at the Autumn Equinox, he is the crucified. His mother, Nu, or Meri, the heaven, seeing her son, the Lord of Terror, greatest of the terrible, setting from the Land of Life, with his hands drooping, she becomes obscure, and there is great darkness over all the land, as at the crucifixion described by Matthew, in which the passing of the Lord of Terror is rendered by the terrible or "loud cry" of the Synoptic version. The Sun-God causes the dead, or those in the earth, to live as he passes down into the under-world, because, as he entered the earth, the tombs were opened, i.e., figuratively. But it is reproduced literally by Matthew.

The death of Osiris, in the Ritual, is followed by the "Night of the Mystery of the Great Shapes," and it is explained that the night of the mystery of the Great Shapes is when there has been made the embalming of the body of Osiris, "the Good Being, justified forever." In the chapter on "the night of the laying-out" of the dead body of Osiris, it is said that "Isis rises on the night of the laying-out of the dead body, to lament over her brother Osiris." And again: "The night of the laying-out" (of the dead Osiris) is mentioned, and again it is described as that on which Isis had risen "to make a wail for her brother."

But this is also the night on which he conquers his enemies, and "receives the birthplace of the Gods." "He tramples on the bandages they make for their burial. He raises his soul, and conceals his body." So the Christ is found to have unwound the linen bandages of burial, and they saw the linen in one place, and the napkin in another. He too conceals his body!

This is closely reproduced, or paralleled, in John's Gospel, where it is Mary Magdalene who rises in the night and comes to the sepulchre, "while it was yet dark," to find the Christ arisen, as the conqueror of death and the grave. In John's version, after the body is embalmed in a hundred pounds weight of spice, consisting of myrrh and aloes, we have the "night of the mystery of the shapes": "For while it was yet dark, Mary Magdalene coming to the sepulchre, and peering in, sees the two angels in white sitting, the one at the head and the other at the feet, where the body had lately lain." And in the chapter of "How a living being is not destroyed in hell, or the hour of life ends not in Hades," there are two youthful Gods — "two youths of light, who prevail as those who see the light," and the vignette shows the deceased walking off. He has risen!

Matthew has only one angel or splendid presence, whose appearance was as lightning, which agrees with Shepi, the Splendid One, who "lights the sarcophagus," as a representative of the divinity, Ra. The risen Christ, who is first seen and recognized by Mary, says to her, "Touch me not, for I am not yet ascended to my Father." The same scene is described by the Gnostics: when Sophia rushes forward to embrace the Christ, he restrains her by exclaiming that he must not be touched.

In the last chapter of the "Preservation of the Body in Hades," there is much mystical matter that looks plainer when written out in John's Gospel. It is said of the regerminated or risen God — "May the Osirian speak to thee?" The Osirian does not know. He (Osiris) knows him. "Let him not grasp him." The Osirified "comes out sound, Immortal is his name." "He has passed along the upper roads" (that is, as a risen spirit).

"He it is who grasps with his hand," and gives the palpable proof of continued personality, as does the Christ, who says, "See my hands and my feet, that it is I myself."

The Sun-God re-arises on the horizon, where he issues forth, "saying to those who belong to his race, Give me your arm." Says the Osirified deceased, "I am made as ye are." "Let him explain it!" At his reappearance the Christ demonstrates that he is made as they are; "See my hands and feet, that it is I myself; handle me and see. And when he had said this he showed them his hands and feet. Then he said to Thomas, Reach hither thy finger, and see my hands, and reach hither thy hand and put it into my side." These descriptions correspond to that of the cut, wounded, and bleeding Sun-God, who says to his companions, "Give me your arm; I am made as ye are."

In the Gospel of the Hebrews he is made to exclaim, "For I am not a bodiless ghost." But in the original, when the risen one says to his companions, "Give me your arm, I am made as ye are," he speaks as a spirit to spirits. Whereas in the Gospels, the Christ has to demonstrate that he is not a spirit, because the scene has been transferred into the earth-life.

The Gnostics truly declared that all the supernatural transactions asserted in the Christian Gospel "were counterparts (or representations) of what took place above." That is, they affirmed the history to be mythical; the celestial allegory made mundane; and they were in the right, as the Egyptian Gospel proves. There are Healers, and Jehoshua Ben-Pandira may have been one. but, because that is possible, we must not allow it to vouch for the impossible! Thus, in the Gospels, the mythical is, and has to be, continually reproduced as miracle. That which naturally pertains to the character of the Sun-God becomes supernatural in appearance when brought down to earth. The Solar God descended into the nether world as the restorer of the bound to liberty, the dead to life. In this region the miracles were wrought, and the transformations took place. The evil spirits and destroying powers were exorcised from the mummies; the halt and the maimed were enabled to get up and go; the dead were raised, a mouth was given to the dumb, and the blind were made to see.

This "reconstruction of the deceased" is transferred to the earth-life, whereupon "the blind receive their sight, and the lame walk, the lepers are cleansed, the deaf hear, and the dead are raised up" at the coming of the Christ, who performed the miracles. The drama, which the Idiotai mistook for human history, was performed by the Sun-God in another world.

I could keep on all day, and all night, or give a dozen lectures, without exhausting my evidence that the Canonical Gospels are only a later literalized réchauffé of the Egyptian writings, the representations in the Mysteries, and the oral teachings of the Gnostics which passed out of Egypt into Greece and Rome — for there is plenty more proof where this comes from. I can but offer a specimen brick of that which is elsewhere a building set four-square, and sound against every blast that blows.

The Christian dispensation is believed to have been ushered in by the birth of a child, and the portrait of that child in the Roman Catacombs as the child of Mary is a youthful Sun-God in the Mummy Image of the child-king, the Egyptian Karast, or Christ. The alleged facts of our Lord's life as Jesus the Christ, were equally the alleged facts of our Lord's life as the Horus of Egypt, whose very name signifies the Lord.

The Christian legends were first related of Horus the Messiah, the Solar Hero, the greatest hero that ever lived in the mind of man — not in the flesh — the only hero to whom the miracles were natural, because he was not human.

From beginning to end the history is not human but divine, and the divine is the mythical. From the descent of the Holy Ghost to overshadow Mary, to the ascension of the risen Christ at the end of forty days, according to the drama of the pre-Christian Mysteries, the subject-matter, the characters, occurrences, events, acts, and sayings bear the impress of the mythical mould instead of the stamp of human history. Right through, the ideas which shape the history were pre-extant, and are identifiably pre-Christian; and so we see the strange sight today in Europe of 100,000,000 of Pagans masquerading as Christians.

Whether you believe it or not does not matter; the fatal fact remains that every trait and feature which go to make up the Christ as Divinity, and every event or circumstance taken to establish the human personality were pre-extant, and pre-applied to the Egyptian and Gnostic Christ, who never could become flesh.

- The Jesus Christ with female paps, who is the Alpha and Omega of Revelation, was the Iu of Egypt, and the Iao of the Chaldeans.
- Jesus as the Lamb of God, and Ichthys the Fish, was Egyptian.
- Jesus as the Coming One;
- Jesus born of the Virgin Mother, who was overshadowed by the Holy Ghost;
- Jesus born of two mothers, both of whose names are Mary;
- Jesus born in the manger — at Christmas, and again at Easter;
- Jesus saluted by the three kings, or Magi;
- Jesus of the transfiguration on the Mount;
- Jesus whose symbol in the Catacombs is the eight-rayed Star — the Star of the East;
- Jesus as the eternal Child;
- Jesus as God the Father, re-born as his own Son;
- Jesus as the Child of twelve years;
- Jesus as the Anointed One of thirty years;
- Jesus in his Baptism;
- Jesus walking on the Waters, or working his Miracles;
- Jesus as the Caster-out of Demons;
- Jesus as Substitute, who suffered in a vicarious atonement for sinful men;
- Jesus whose followers are the two brethren, the four fishers, the seven fishers, the twelve apostles, the seventy (or seventy-two in some texts) whose names were written in Heaven;
- Jesus who was administered to by seven women;
- Jesus in his bloody sweat;
- Jesus betrayed by Judas;
- Jesus as conqueror of the grave;
- Jesus the Resurrection and the Life;
- Jesus before Herod;
- In the Hades, and in his re-appearance to the women, and to the seven fishers;
- Jesus who was crucified both on the 14th and 15th of the month Nisan;
- Jesus who was also crucified in Egypt (as it is written in Revelation);
- Jesus as judge of the dead, with the sheep on the right hand, and the goats on the left, is Egyptian from first to last, in every phase, from the beginning to the end;

MAKE WHATSOEVER YOU CAN OF JEHOSHUA BEN-PANDIRA

In some of the ancient Egyptian Temples the Christian iconoclasts, when tired of hacking and hewing at the symbolic figures incised in the chambers of imagery, and defacing the most prominent features of the monuments, found they could not dig out the hieroglyphics and took to covering them over with plaster or tempera; and this plaster, intended to hide the meaning and stop the mouth of the stone Word, has served to preserve the ancient writings, as fresh in hue and sharp in outline as when they were first cut and colored.

In a similar manner the Temple of the ancient religion was invaded, and possession gradually gained by connivance of Roman power; and that the enduring fortress, not built, but quarried out of the solid rock, was stuccoed all over the front, and made white awhile with its look of brand-newness, and re-opened under the sign of another name — that of the carnalized Christ. And all the time each nook and corner were darkly alive with the presence and the proofs of the earlier gods, and the pre-Christian origins, even though the hieroglyphics remained unread until the time of Champollion! But stucco is not for lasting wear, it cracks and crumbles; sloughs off and slinks away into its natal insignificance; the rock is the sole true foundation; the rock is the only record in which we can reach reality at last!

Wilkinson, the Egyptologist, has actually said of Osiris on earth: — "Some may be disposed to think that the Egyptians, being aware of the promises of the real saviour, had anticipated that event, regarding it as though it had already happened, and introduced that mystery into their religious system!" This is what obstetrists term a false presentation; a birth feet-foremost. We are also told by writers on the Catacombs, and the Christian Iconography, that this figure is Osiris, as a type of Christ. This is Pan, Apollo, Aristeus, as a type of Christ. This is Harpocrates, as a type of Christ. This is Mercury, but as a type of Christ; this is the devil (for Sut-Mercury was the devil), as a type of Christ; until long hearing of the facts reversed, perverted and falsified, makes one feel as if under a nightmare which has lasted for eighteen centuries, knowing the Truth to have been buried alive and made dumb all that time; and believing that it has only to get voice and make itself heard to end the lying once for all, and bring down the curtain of oblivion at last upon the most pitiful drama of delusion ever witnessed on the human stage.

And here the worst foes of the truth have ever been, and still are, the rationalizers of the Mythos, such as the Unitarians. They have assumed the human history as the starting point, and accepted the existence of a personal founder of Christianity as the one initial and fundamental fact. They have done their best to humanize the divinity of the Mythos, by discharging the supernatural and miraculous element, in order that the narrative might be accepted as history. Thus they have lost the battle from the beginning, by fighting it on the wrong ground.

The Christ is
- A popular lay-figure that never lived, and
- A lay-figure of Pagan origin;
- A lay-figure that was once the Ram, and afterwards the Fish;
- A lay-figure that in human form was the portrait and image of a dozen different gods.

The imagery of the Catacombs shows that the types there represented are not the ideal figures of the human reality! They are the sole reality for six or seven centuries after A.D., because they had been so in the centuries long before. There is no man upon the cross in the Catacombs of Rome for seven hundred years! The symbolism, the allegories, the figures, and types, brought on by the Gnostics, remained there just what they had been to the Romans, Greeks, Persians, and Egyptians. Yet the dummy ideal of Paganism is supposed to have become doubly real as the God who was made flesh, to save mankind from the impossible "fall!" Remember that the primary foundation-stone for a history in the New Testament is dependent upon the Fall of Man being a fact in the Old; whereas it was only a fable, which had its own mythical and unhistorical meaning.

When we try over again that first step once taken in the dark, we find no foothold for us, because there was no stair. The Fall is absolutely non-historical, and, consequently, the first bit of standing-ground for an actual Christ, the redeemer, is missing in the very beginning. Any one who set up, or was set up, for an historical Savior from a non-historical Fall, could only be an historical impostor. But the Christ of the Gospels is not even that! He is in no sense an historical personage. It is impossible to establish the existence of an historical character, even as an impostor. For such a one the two witnesses — Astronomical Mythology and Gnosticism — completely prove an alibi forever! From the first supposed catastrophe to the final one, the figures of the celestial allegory were ignorantly mistaken for matters of fact, and thus the orthodox Christolator is left at last to climb to heaven with one foot resting on the ground of a fall that is fictitious, and the other foot on the ground of a redemption that must be fallacious. It is a fraud founded on a fable!

Every time the Christian turns to the East to bow his obeisance to the Christ, it is a confession that the cult is Solar, the admission being all the more fatal because it is unconscious. Every picture of the Christ, with the halo of glory, and the accompanying Cross of the Equinox, proffers proof.

The Christian doctrine of a resurrection furnishes evidence, absolutely conclusive, of the Astronomical and Kronian nature of the origins! This is to occur, as it always did, at the end of a cycle; or at the end of the world! Christian Revelation knows nothing of immortality, except in the form of periodic renewal, dependent on the "Coming One", and the resurrection of the dead still depends on the day of judgment and the last day, at the end of the world! They have no other world. Their only other world is at the end of this.

Now there are no fools living who would be fools big enough to cross the Atlantic Ocean in a barque so rotten and unseaworthy as this in which they hope to cross the dark River of Death, and, on a pier of cloud, be landed safe in Heaven. The Christian Theology was responsible for substituting faith instead of knowledge; and the European mind is only just beginning to recover from the mental paralysis induced by that doctrine which came to its natural culmination in the Dark Ages.

The Christian religion is responsible for enthroning the cross of death in heaven, with a deity on it, doing public penance for a private failure in the commencement of creation. It has taught men to believe that the vilest spirit may be washed white, in the atoning blood of the purest, offered up as a bribe to an avenging God. It has divinized a figure of helpless human suffering, and a face of pitiful pain; as if there were naught but a great heartache at the core of all things; or the vast Infinite were but a veiled and sad-eyed sorrow that brings visibly to birth in the miseries of human life. But "in the old Pagan world men deified the beautiful, the glad;" as they will again, upon a loftier pedestal, when the fable of this fictitious fall of man, and false redemption by the cloud-begotten God, has passed away like a phantasm of the night, and men awake to learn that they are here to wage ceaseless war upon sordid suffering, remediable wrong, and preventable pain; here to put an end to them, not to apotheosize an effigy of Sorrow to be adored as a type of the Eternal. For the beneficent is the most beautiful; the happiest are the healthiest; the most Godlike is most glad. The Christian Cult has fanatically fought for its false theory, and waged incessant warfare against Nature and Evolution — Nature's intention made somewhat visible — and against some of the noblest instincts, during eighteen centuries. Seas of human blood have been spilt to keep the barque of Peter afloat. Earth has been honeycombed with the graves of the martyrs of Freethought. Heaven has been filled with a horror of great darkness in the name of God.

Eighteen centuries are a long while in the life-time of a lie, but a brief span in the eternity of Truth. The Fiction is sure to be found out, and the Lie will fall at last! At last!! At last !!!

> No matter though it towers to the sky,
> And darkens earth, you cannot make the lie
> Immortal; though stupendously enshrined
> By art in every perfect mould of mind:
> Angelo, Rafael, Milton, Handel, all
> Its pillars, cannot stay it from the fall.
> The Pyramid of Imposture reared by Rome,
> All of cement, for an eternal home,
> Must crumble back to earth, and every gust
> Shall revel in the desert of its dust;
> And when the prison of the Immortal, Mind,
> Hath fallen to set free the bound and blind,
> No more shall life be one long dread of death;
> Humanity shall breathe with ampler breath,
> Expand in spirit, and in stature rise,
> To match its birthplace of the earth and skies.

THE STELLAR CULT
BY PAUL TICE

The Stellar cult originated in Egypt. Much of it was to merge later with Christianity.

The God Horus

The major deity of the Stellar Cult was Horus, who signified the horizon. The Egyptian god Horus was known as the Great Chief of the Ax or the Great God of the Ax. He was symbolized by an ax or double ax, sometimes symbolized by a hammer. Horus, the Egyptian god, was also referred to as the "God of the Double Horizon." The first Temple of the Ax was built at Edfu, where Horus was also named the "Lord of the Forged City." The Temple of Edfu was oriented north from a point within the Little Bear constellation. An inscription found there says,

> I cast my face towards
>> the course of the rising constellations.
> I let my glance enter
>> the constellation of the Great Bear.
> I established
>> the four corners of my temple.

This was something presumably said by Horus about the nature or the placement of this important temple at Edfu. This temple, meant to worship Horus, god of the Ax, was nothing new in relation to other parts of the world. This god of the Ax, as part of the world-wide Stellar cult, has been found in other areas of the world such as Tepoxtecatl, god of the Ax of the Mexicans. Also there is Uracocha, god of the Ax from Tinogasta. The Toltec god of the Ax was also found to be from the area of Tepozteco.

Evidence seems to indicate that the first exodus of the Stellar cult people to arrive in America from Egypt via Asia did end up in Mexico. Tollan, another common name in Mexico and even the name of a city, is also another name for Horus.

We also find the god of the Ax named Ramman. He is of the Chaldeans. Then there is the god of the Ax found with the Susians. The list goes on and on from around the world in finding the common god of the Ax who originated in the Stellar cult.

One of the earliest Stellar cults for Horus was commonly called the Cult of Aten, or disk worship. This disk worship, sometimes portrayed as a winged disk, was mistakenly interpreted as the sun, according to Albert Churchward, by many Egyptologists. In fact, this disk was originally a symbol for Aten, which in turn was a very early name of Horus as god of the dual horizons. The word "Aten" is in fact derived from an ancient name for the child Horus.

Horus is the earliest form of Aten and is symbolically portrayed as the winged disk. This winged disk has also traveled the world and in one example it is found above the door of a temple at Ocosingo which is near Palenque in Mexico. It is also known as the Thunderbird by North American Indian tribes. It also has been found as far away as Scotland at a place called Vitrified Fort in Ainworth.

The Assyrians and Chaldeans displayed winged disks showing that this Stellar cult was carried into these countries as well. The Stellar cult was the earliest of the three cults: Solar, Lunar and Stellar. It lasted a very long time in Egypt, so it is much harder to trace the origins of this particular cult than the other two. What makes it difficult to trace is that when the Lunar and Solar cults followed, if they could not kill all the old Stellar cult people, as they did in Europe, they grafted some of their new doctrines onto the Stellar cults, so the local religion became a hodgepodge of various Egyptian beliefs. There is no doubt that scientific research proves this today.

During the advent of the Lunar cult, there were various episodes of exodus — people leaving the Egyptian area who were Stellar cult people. When they left the motherland they took with them the doctrines that had evolved up to the time of the Exodus, and many were cut off from the progress that was constantly taking place in Egypt. They moved on and remained in their primary Stellar religious phase. This is why researchers find, in that general area of the Middle East, varying concepts and examples of the Stellar cults. Tracing them back to their earliest times has been the researcher's true challenge. Horus represents the earliest known part of the Stellar cult that we have been able to determine.

Out of the many countries that the Stellar cults moved into, let us use Japan as one example. Of all the Shinto gods of the heavens the highest one is said to dwell in the star Tai-yah of the constellation Draco, also known as the constellation of Horus-Sebeck, the Crocodile Dragon. The Chinese also recognized a Stellar enclosure or circle of stars in the northern heavens in the region of Draco and Ursa Minor. They named this circle of stars after the other lower deities who surround the sovereign or most high.

The Egyptians had this very same setup. The circle of the seven lords of eternity was first, with the throne of the highest erected in the center. According to the mystery of the seven stars in the book of Revelation (1:16, 20), the seven as servants are depicted around the throne of God. There may be a strong connection here as well.

Jesus is accompanied by the seven great angels or spirits, who are the stars, whose place is before the throne of God. Being of Egyptian origin, these were originally the seven servants or the "Seshu" of Horus.

The God Set

The Stellar cult mainly followed Horus, but within it were also the followers of Set or Seth. Set was the firstborn child of the Great Mother Apt and between Set and the Crocodile Dragon Horus, the two of them formed the primary dyad that is sometimes called "Set-Typhon," or in Egyptian "Set-Tept." According to one account of the book of Genesis, Set was the firstborn child of Eve. He was the primary ruler and symbolized as the male hippopotamus. As the primary power he was the first to sit at the pole of heaven. This is why he was the reputed author of astronomy.

Horus and Set

Getting back to the two main Stellar cults of Horus and Set, these two were constantly at odds with each other throughout the mythological history of Egypt, therefore you cannot have one without the other. The two did in fact start at approximately the same time. Followers of Horus and those of Set fought many battles which were actually fights in the domain of fact, and therefore not mythical. Although the two cults were started at approximately the same time, the cult of Set started a bit earlier than the cult of Horus.

Religion itself did not evolve until the Horus cult evolved. It was the followers of Horus who could express themselves well and they were able to keep the records of the past.

Besides the hawk, the head of the eagle is one of the symbols of Horus. The same symbolism is found in Christianity where St. John is imaged symbolically by the eagle. The Stellar cults were the first groups to keep track of time in any sophisticated sort of way. Before the Stellar cult there was no record of time except night and day, and the wet season and dry season. With the advent of the Stellar cult they began working on astronomical and mathematical knowledge and they worked it out to a very high state. The high state which they had attained is proved by the Great Pyramid of Giza, something never equaled to this day.

The main subject of the Stellar cult was the history of Horus. His title was that of Repa. It identified him as the child born to be king. Horus had as his mother one who had begotten him, but yet she was a virgin. Therefore Horus was referred to as "the bastard." (In the legend of Jesus, to the Jews he was also called the Mainzer or "bastard.") Horus the child on various papyri is pictured on his mother's lap and is representative of the resurrection and renewal of life for another year.

Horus and Apap

Horus came to Egypt as a savior of the people. He saved them from the dreaded drought. He came invested with "the power of the Southern Lakes." This power was meant to drown the dragon in the inundation, as this dragon was the opposite or antagonist of Horus. Horus is a savior because he is the bringer of much-needed water. He also treads the serpent of darkness underfoot and is therefore referred to as the renewer of light (the same as Jesus).

This reptile that opposed Horus was represented in the constellation of Hydra and the reptile's name was Apap. It is the fearsome monster that in the various Egyptian legends drank up all the water. In the Solar cult, Apap is the antagonist of Ra and is referred to as the blind, devouring darkness, but as the adversary of Horus, Apap or Hydra is the dragon of drought. Drought in the land of Egypt was their major curse and the evil dragon was its deadly image. So this was a physical evil, not a moral one.

Horus was interpreted as being born of the great Southern Fish and was represented also as the fish man who came to Egypt with water. This water was portrayed as a river in the heavens. It traveled north from the south up to the foot of Orion. In the earlier Stellar cult Horus as Orion was the hunter of the power of darkness with his dogs Cyon and Prokyon. The power of darkness was represented by Apap the Dragon. The particular time of year when this victory was said to have taken place occurred as Orion rose in the Scorpion constellation. This took place in the southern heavens, and when Orion rose up he bruised the serpent's head or crushed the Dragon underfoot and this is when Apap is put into bonds. He is cut up piecemeal and submerged in the green lake of heaven. This was an important time to the Egyptians. It also represented the victory of Horus over Set. However, the Stellar cult at this time of year celebrated the victory of Horus over Apap (as opposed to Set). This was the beginning of a new year for the Egyptians.

The Fish and the Virgin

The virgin mother of Horus was known as Neith and she was represented in the Stellar cult by a white vulture. Once again Horus was known to be her offspring. His birth also represented the incorporation of a spirit of light that had entered into human beings. In Christian doctrines this same vulture is symbolized as a pelican who had pierced her own thigh to give her blood to her young for nourishment. Blood is considered by many to have the spirit of life within it. This pelican represents the earliest soul considered to be human, being born of the mother blood. The soul that was made flesh was the child Horus.

The origin of a Savior coming as a little child is traced to the child Horus. He brought new life to Egypt every year. Horus, before being known as human, was symbolized as Ichthus, the fish. Later the image of Horus represented the young god in Solar form as the cause of creation. In his more primitive version this fish as Horus symbolized the soul of life, or food, ascending up from the water of vegetation. It was like a spring of water welling up from the depths beneath the earth to furnish food and other edible plants within the reeds and other swampy areas of the Egyptian river valleys. It was within this area of the reeds, according to the Egyptian legends, that light first broke out of darkness in the beginning during the domain of Set. This is where the twin children of darkness and light were born. Those twin children were Set, of darkness, and Horus, of light. This very same legend can be found the world over — in Japan, North America, and various other cultures around the world. You can go to practically any of them and find this same story. Wherever you find this story it can definitely be traced to the original Horus of the Stellar cult.

In Christian gnostic doctrines you find stories of Ichthus the fish. Horus was the earliest fish man known in mythology. He referred to himself as "the fish in the form of a man." The Australian aborigines also have an interesting story about a gigantic frog who drinks up all the waters in the world. This frog, of course, represents Apap the monster who swallows the waters at sundown. The Andaman islanders also have a story about a conflict between the bird of light and the devil of darkness. This devil of darkness also drinks up the waters and is represented by a very large toad. The Iroquois Indians of North America have the same myth as well, showing a huge devouring monster as a giant frog. This same story is found in different aboriginal tribes in the Lake Tyres area. In Mexico this large water-drinking creature is represented by a snake.

The True Savior?

It is only Horus throughout the world, or his representing deity throughout each culture, that is able to save the world from this lack of water. This Stellar cult doctrine had been carried out of Egypt. That is the root of this story. Set and the evil serpent Apap are synonymous. In some Egyptian reliefs Horus is depicted as an elephant. He is standing with great weight upon the head of the evil serpent Apap with his foot crushing down on its head and preventing it from drinking all the water of the world. At the same time he is pouring water, symbolizing rain, out of a large jug of water to fertilize the earth. Another Egyptian relief shows the great Apap, after having swallowed the water and the light of the world, and Horus (shown once again as an elephant god) fighting him to make him disgorge the water and the light. In yet another culture this story is found in India where the Naga is a very powerful and great god seen as a cobra. This is representative of the deity Horus. In India, Asia, and even in Central America, we do find elephant depictions in various important pictographs that have great religious significance. This elephant was carried to these cultures as a symbol of Horus.

Symbols in the Sky

When we look to the sky we find clear symbols of not only the bringing of water after it has been drunk up by the evil demon, but of other legends as well.

We find that the river flowing at its highest source in the sky was depicted by the Milky Way. The mother goddess gives forth the milk that is within this river which gives life to Horus. Horus is shown feeding at the breast of his mother in many Egyptian reliefs on temples. It seems Horus in turn is able to bring this life-giving liquid to the earth in time of need.

The stars were extremely important to the Egyptians. What could be the earliest form of astrology is found within the Stellar cult of Egypt. They divided the heavens into two different divine circles, the north and south circles of heaven. Each of these divine circles was divided into twelve houses with separate and distinct markings for each one represented by different animals. These animals symbolized the twelve great spirits of Egypt. Horus was known as the Lord of the Spirits in the Heaven of Eternity.

The Solar cult, which came later, was the one that originated the zodiac as we know it today, but this earlier Stellar arrangement was not only the predecessor, but seems to be the entire basis for the zodiacal system of the Solar cult. In fact the Solar cult did later use the same original twelve characters that were used by the Stellar cult. The names of the original characters used in the Solar cult came from the Stellar cult. Those twelve were:

1. Set	4. Hapi	7. Amsta	10. Atum
2. Horus	5. Ap-Uat	8. Anup	11. Sau
3. Shu	6. Kabhsenuf	9. Ptah	12. Hu

The four brothers of Horus composed four out of this divine circle of twelve. This original twelve was for the southern hemisphere. As stated earlier, they had divided the heavens into two regions, north and south, each with its own divine circle. The south came first and later transferred the same system to the northern heavens. The very uppermost part of the northern heavens was symbolized by a mountain summit or a pyramid, or sometimes as a mound of earth, a papyrus plant or a lotus in the water of immensity.

Throughout the World

To recap, we find Horus in virtually every culture around the world. Horus was, and is, the entire basis for the Stellar cult. He is, however, absent in the Mayan and Incan cultures because they were Solar cult people for the most part. The Stellar cults in the new world were found in the other ancient Mexican cultures such as the Toltecs and the Zapotecs. The Zapotecs knew Horus as Pelle-Nij. This name meant "the Great Morning Star," or the Lord of the Dawn. This clearly was the same as the Egyptian Horus. They knew Set, the god of darkness and the underworld, as Tepeolotlec. All the gods of the Zapotecs were typical of the old Stellar cult. The first three born of their mother goddess Ta-Urt represented in all of their characteristics Set, Horus and Shu.

Out of the three cults — Stellar, Lunar and Solar — the Stellar cult forms the basis of many of the two later forms of worship. Even so, the rankings of importance are all similar, since each has provided what we now know today as being important parts of our entire religious systems throughout the world. We cannot know our religions of the world today without knowing of each of these three separate cults. They all provide separate and important parts of what we know today. Although they functioned separately during each time that they were exhibiting their power over the world, they work collectively today and function more as a unit, although that was never originally intended.

THE LUNAR CULT
BY PAUL TICE

The Lunar cult followed the Stellar cult. This was at a point when time itself was kept track of by the moon, rather than the stars. I tend to think that some knowledge was lost, because in order to reckon time by using the stars, I believe, you must have a more advanced system of things. Looking up at the moon and determining cycles by the moon alone was a rather easy process compared to using the stars. For example the Stellar cult was able to determine the length of the Great Year which lasted in cycles of 25,827 years. You cannot do this by using the moon alone.

Hathor: Divine Mother

The child Horus was now considered in the Lunar cult as being brought forth by Hathor. She was most commonly represented as a cow and was the mother goddess. She was also the mother of generation, childbirth, and maternity. When she was depicted in human form she carried the Ankh in her right hand and a staff in her left. She was crowned with the double horns with the moon's crescent wedged in between.

When depicted as a cow, she was seen as wearing this same headgear. In the legends she is also considered a virgin. In the Babylonian story the same Great Mother is known as Ishtar. She represented the moon. She descends through seven gates on her downward way to the underworld. She is stripped of all her glory as she comes down to fetch light and the water of life from the lower regions, thereby giving rebirth to vegetation in the upper world. In describing the Egyptian mysteries Plutarch tells us that on the eve of the winter solstice the Egyptians were known to carry the cow seven times around the temple. This was a model for the seeking of Horus by Hathor. Horus was the savior by water, and the earth-mother was in great distress for the need of water in the wintertime. It was on the eve of the winter solstice when this particular Egyptian mystery ritual took place.

Horus/Khensu: Divine Son

Hathor's child, Horus, was usually represented by one of two animals, either a golden calf or a golden hawk. Nowadays most of us know Horus as being in the image of a hawk. The Milky Way provided the celestial water of heaven, then called milk. It flowed from the cow of heaven to the child Horus who is commonly shown as at Hathor's breast. So it is clear that this cult of the great mother and her child was brought out of the Stellar cult into the Lunar. There are only slight variations in change, but that is where it originated.

The image of Horus continues on from the Stellar cult into the Lunar cult in the form of Khensu. The word Khensu is synonymous with travel, moving about, or to run. As the moon god, this was appropriate. The Lunar cult has transformed Horus into the Moon, away from Stellar cult symbolism. He was the great lord of heaven. Through his power he caused women to conceive, cattle to become fertile and the smallest germ in the egg to grow. He caused to shine upon the earth the light of the crescent moon. During the new moon he was envisioned as a fiery bull. The most common depiction of him shows him with the hawk head of Horus crowned with the lunar disk on top. The disk is quite often resting in another moon symbol, a crescent, which looks like two horns. In Egyptian texts, Khensu was referred to as the second great light in the heavens. Following the sun, the moon is precisely that. Khensu was the son of Amen. Amen was also known to the Egyptians as the sun god Ra.

Cosmic Timekeeping

It seems that the reason the Stellar cult evolved from the Lunar cult was human error. In the Stellar cult there developed a failure in keeping time so there was needed a new heaven, the lunar heaven, which followed in order for people to keep track of time better.

Taht was appointed supreme timekeeper. He was also known to other cultures as Hermes. The moon in the shape of a crescent looks like the symbol of two horns. It was commonly depicted upon the heads of gods. It actually symbolized a boat or the ark of Taht. That is why they put the full moon inside this so-called boat — because two symbols of the moon made little sense. The crescent moon was known as "the ark of the Lord of Light upon the waters of the night." This ark sailed through the sky at night above the dark waters. In the biblical story of Noah's ark the people were saved from flooding with that particular ark. It was the same case with the Egyptian ark. Flooding at a certain time of year was important to the Egyptians. That is why the crescent moon was symbolized by the ark, because the people were saved from flooding every year by the god.

Lunar Symbols

The two gods Horus and Set continued their duality in the Lunar cult. Each represented two different phases of the moon. Set was the dark half and Horus was the light half. One represented the waxing and one the waning of the moon.

In the Lunar cult we have, for the first time, represented as the slayer of the evil dragon the woman, or mother goddess. It was the son of the mother goddess who helped her in this process as more of a follower than the slayer himself.

One of the animals that represents the moon to us today is the hare or the rabbit. This hare was actually preceded in Egypt by both the frog and the grasshopper. These represented the moon to the Egyptians because of the light that leapt up into a fresh place every night. This is why still today certain African tribes have leaping dances during the phases of the new moon. Of course the hare, which did become later the symbol of the moon, is another great leaper.

The cat is another great Egyptian symbol of the moon, because it could see in the dark: it could see at night. This was much like the moon that saw by night and kept watch in the dark.

She was the mother goddess who destroyed the devouring monster. She was known as the lady of light representing the very bright part of the moon. This same legend is found in India where Indra slays the serpent of darkness. This serpent was thought to be the swallower of light. Once the slaying was successful, the waters of heaven, meaning the waters of life, rushed forth. This could almost be a female version of the Set-Horus conflict.

The highest god of the Lunar cult was Taht-Kahemen. He is worshipped as the "only-one." He is the same as Horus. Taht-Kahemen is linguistically similar to the Egyptian pharaoh Tutenkamen.

The Great Year

The Great Year was composed of more than 25,000 years, according to Egyptian reckoning. They have the pole of the earth's axis changing seven times during this period. The human birthplace changes each time the location of the pole changes. During each new creation the pole sinks into the waters and all are drowned. Out of the seven deluges one great deluge ends it all. So ends the Great Year of 25,827 years.

The unit of measure at this time was the cubit. If you recall from the book of Genesis, God gave it as a unit of measure. The seven different resting places of the pole within the great year were celebrated and ritualized by the Egyptians at Abydos and Memphis. The ritual involved carrying around the Taht-Cross to the seven different symbolized resting places that marked each of the stations of the pole. This ritual is now found in modern Christianity in the ceremony of the seven stations of the cross. This Christian ceremony retraces the seven resting places of the cross on the way to Calvary. During each of these seven periods of the Great

Year there were seven different rulers of the world. These seven were the Uranographic figures in the Stellar cult and referred to as the Seven Lords and Masters of Eternity. In the Lunar cult they represent the seven wise masters of arts and science.

These seven to the Egyptians were (1) Set, (2) Sebek-Horus, (3) Shu, (4) Hapi, (5) Tuamutef, (6) Kabhsenuf, and (7) Amsta. These were the same seven who were considered to have caused the deluge in the Babylonian legend. They go by different names in Babylon. They are also found under different names in the Book of Enoch.

The Bow of Heaven

Here is another biblical parallel. The crescent moon of Thoth was a representation of the bow in heaven. This was a sign that there should be no further deluge of destruction. The deluge in the Stellar cult was now over, being defeated and destroyed through the agency of the Lunar goddess Hathor. So the Bow of Thoth was said to be put in heaven under the promise that the waters should never again cover the earth. The Hebrew text in the Old Testament contains this exact same story, but inserts the name of Yahweh. Most people interpret this bow of heaven in the Old Testament to mean a rainbow, but it was actually the crescent moon. This was not to mean that the moon was created at this time, it meant that they were moving from the stellar process of keeping time to the lunar. It is said that Anup failed to keep correct time in the Stellar phase and let in the deluge. This was now to be avoided by moving to lunar time, that is, keeping track of time monthly as opposed to stellar time that kept track on yearly cycles.

This lunar crescent was not only the bow of the deluge which was promising no more destruction for the future, but it was also the ark of safety representing the boat of protection from the floodwaters. This was just one example of the many, many Bible stories which have come from far older legends.

The Moon before the Sun

In the Turin Papyrus of the Egyptians it is said of the Lunar god Taht,

> He hath made all that the world contains
> and hath given it light when all was darkness.
> There was as yet no sun.

This means that there was no sun as a representative of time. For the Lunar cults this was a new creation. The first creation of time was Stellar time. The second creation was Lunar time. The third creation was the Solar cult that had not yet come into being.

In Genesis of our Bible the sun is created before the moon. In the Babylonian account of creation the moon is produced before the sun. This is because of the order of these timekeeping cults. This proves that the Lunar cult was known in Babylonia before the Hebrew Solar version came into existence.

In the Lunar cult it was clear that the imagery was different from that of the Stellar cult, but their beliefs and religious ideas were basically the same. The Stellar, followed by the Lunar cult, offers us a very clear vision of the origin and evolution of religious ideas. It is now time to see how the Lunar cult evolved into the Solar cult. The Solar cult, as it emerged, formed the strongest foundations to our modern belief systems. There is no better person capable of explaining this than Jordan Maxwell.

SCRIPTURAL REFERENCES

1. Light of the World

And this is the condemnation that
light is come into the world,
and men loved darkness rather than light,
because their deeds were evil.

John 3:19

Then spake Jesus again unto them, saying,
I am the light of the world:
he that followeth me shall not walk in darkness,
but shall have the light of the world.

John 8:12

As long as I am in the World,
I am the light of the world.

John 9:5

2. Risen Sun

But after **I am risen again**,
I will go before you unto Galilee.

Matt 26:32

He is not here:
for **he is risen**, as he said.
Come, see the place where the Lord lay.
And go quickly, and tell his disciples
that **he is risen from the dead**;
and, behold, he goeth before you into Galilee;
there shall ye see him:
lo, I have told you.

Matt 28:6–7

To give light to them that sit in darkness
and in the shadow of death,
to guide our feet into the way of peace.

Luke 1:79

The people which sat in darkness **saw great light**;
and to them which sat in the region
and shadow of death **light is sprung up**.

Matt 4:16

3. God, Heavenly Fire

For **the Lord Thy God is a consuming fire**,
even a jealous God.

Deut 4:24

For **our God is a consuming fire**.

Heb 12:29

4. Heaven

And no man hath **ascended up to heaven**,
but he **that came down from heaven**,
even the Son of man **which is in heaven**.

John 3:13

For **I came down from heaven**,
>> not to do mine own will,
> but the will of him that sent me.

>> *John 6:38*

> See that ye refuse not him that speaketh.
> For if they escaped not
>> who refused him that spake on earth,
> much more shall not we escape,
> if we turn away from him
>> **that speaketh from heaven**.

>> *Heb 12:25*

5. Father Glorified in Sun

> Jesus saith unto him,
>> Have I been so long time with you,
>> and yet have you not known me, Philip?
>> **He that hath seen me hath seen the Father**;
>> and how sayest thou then,
>>> Show us the Father?

>> *John 14:9*

> For God,
>> who commanded the light to **shine out of darkness**,
> hath shined in our hearts,
>> to give **the light of the knowledge**
>>> **of the glory of God**
>> in the face of Jesus Christ.

>> *2 Cor 4:6*

> And that every tongue should confess
>> that **Jesus Christ is Lord**,
>> **to the glory of God the Father**.

>> *Phil 2:11*

6. Our Savior

> And said unto the woman,
>> Now we believe, not because of thy saying;
>>> for we have heard him ourselves,
>>> and know that this is indeed the Christ
>>> **the Savior of the World**.

>> *John 4:42*

> And we have seen and do testify
>> that **the Father sent the Son**
>> to be **the Saviour of the world**.

>> *I John 4:14*

7. Sun Gives His Life

> Even as **the Son of man came**
>> not to be ministered unto,
> but to minister,
>> and **to give his life** a ransom for many.

>> *Matt 20:28*

For even **the Son of man came**
> not to be ministered unto,
but to minister,
> and **to give his life** a ransom for many.

Mark 10:45

8. Risen Savior Will Come Again

And if I go and prepare a place for you,
> I will **come again**,
and receive you unto myself;
> that where I am, there ye may be also.

John 14:3

He which testifieth these things saith,
> Surely **I come quickly**. Amen.
Even so, **come, Lord Jesus**.

Rev 22:20

9. God So Loved the World

For **God so loved the world**,
> that he gave his only begotten Son,
that whosoever believeth in him should not perish,
> but have everlasting life.

John 3:16

In this was manifested the **love of God** toward us,
> because that **God sent his only begotten Son**
> into the world,
that he might live through him.

I John 4:9

10. Works of Darkness

The night is far spent,
> the day is at hand;
let us therefore cast off the **works of darkness**,
> and let us put on the armour of light.

Rom 13:12

And have no fellowship
> with the unfruitful **works of darkness**,
but rather reprove them.

Eph 5:11

11. Prince of Peace

And killed the **Prince of life**,
> whom God raised from the dead;
whereof we are witnesses.

Acts 3:15

To whom also Abraham gave a tenth part of all;
> first being by interpretation King of righteousness,
> and after that also King of Salem,
> which is, **King of peace**.

Heb 7:2–3

For unto us a child is born, unto us a son is given:
and the government shall be upon his shoulder:
and his name shall be called
>Wonderful,
>Counsellor,
>the Mighty God,
>the everlasting Father,
>the **Prince of Peace**.

Isa 9:6

12. Prince of Darkness

But the Pharisees said,
>He casteth out devils
>>through the **prince of the devils**.

Matt 9:34

For it is a shame even to speak of those things
>which are done of them in secret.

Eph 6:12

Take heed therefore that the **light** which is in thee
is not **darkness**.
>hath delivered us
>>from the **power of darkness**, and
>hath translated us
>>into the kingdom of his dear Son.

Col 1:13

To open their eyes,
>and to turn them **from darkness** to light,
>and from **the power of Satan** unto God . . .

Acts 26:18

13. Light was Good — Darkness was Bad

The light of the body is the eye;
>therefore when thine eye is single,
thy whole body also is full of light;
>but when thine eye is **evil**,
>thy body also is **full of darkness**.

Luke 11:34

And this is the condemnation,
>that light is come into the world, and
>**men loved darkness** rather than light,
>>**because their deeds were evil**.
For everyone that doeth **evil hateth the light**,
>neither cometh to the light,
>>lest their **deeds** should **be reproved**.
But he that doeth truth cometh to the light,
>that his **deeds** may be **made manifest**,
>that they are **wrought in God**.

John 3:19–21

For we wrestle not against flesh and blood, but,
    against principalities,
    against powers,
    against the **rulers of the darkness
      of this world**,
    against **spiritual wickedness** in high places.

Eph 6:12

God is light, and in him is **no darkness** at all

1 John 1:5

14. I Am the Light and Truth

In him was life;
    and the life was **the light of men**.

John 1:4

Jesus saith unto him,
    I am the way, the truth and the life:
    no man cometh unto the Father,
      but by me.

John 14:6

15. Giving Thanks to the Father

But **thanks be to God**,
which giveth us the victory
    through our Lord Jesus Christ.

1 Cor 15:57

Now **thanks be unto God**,
    which always causeth us to **triumph in Christ**,
    and maketh **manifest the savior** of his knowledge
      by us in every place.

2 Cor 2:14

And whatsoever ye do in word or deed,
    do all in the **name of the Lord Jesus**,
    giving **thanks to God**
      and **the Father by him**.

Col 3:17

16. Two Brothers

Then was **Jesus** led up
    of the spirit into the wilderness
    to be tempted of **the devil**.

Matt 4:1

And the Lord commended the unjust steward,
    because he had done wisely:
    for the **children of this world**
      are in their generation wiser
    than the **children of light**.

Luke 16:8

Be ye not unequally yoked together with unbelievers:
for what fellowship hath righteousness
with unrighteousness?
and what communion hath **light**
with darkness?

2 Cor 6:14

17. New Born Babe / Savior

And the daughter of Pharaoh came down
to wash at the river;
. . . and when she saw the ark among the flags,
she sent her maid to fetch it.
And when she opened it,
she saw the child . . .
She called his name **Moses**:
and she said,
"because I drew him out of the water. "

Exodus 2:5–6, 10

And **Moses** was learned
in **all the wisdom of the Egyptians**,
and was mighty
in words and deeds.

Acts 7:22

"Arise,
and take the young child
and his mother,
and flee **into Egypt**" . . .
When he arose,
he took the young child
and his mother by night,
and **departed into Egypt**:
. . . that it might be fulfilled
which was spoken of the Lord
by the prophet saying,
"Out of Egypt I have called my son."

Matt 2:13–15

18. Doves and Hawks

And straightway coming out of the water,
he saw the **heavens opened**, and
the Spirit **like a dove** descending upon him.

Mark 1:10 (see also Matt 3:16,
Luke 3:22, John 1:32)

Doth the **hawk** fly by thy wisdom,
and stretch her wings toward the south?

Job 39:26

19. Born Again

Jesus answered and said unto him,
Verily, verily, I say unto thee,
except **a man be born again**,
he cannot see the kingdom of God.
Jesus answered,
Verily, Verily, I say unto thee,
Except **a man be born of water
and of the Spirit**,
he cannot enter into the kingdom of God.
Marvel not that I said unto the,
Ye must be born again.

John 3:3, 5 & 7

Being born again,
not of corruptible seed,
but of incorruptible,
by the Word of God,
which liveth and abideth forever.

I Pet 1:23

20. Sun Dies, World Left in the Dark

And it was about the sixth hour,
and there was a **darkness over all the earth**
until the ninth hour.

Luke 23:44–45
(see also Mk 15:33)

. . . for what fellowship hath **righteousness
with unrighteousness**?
and what communion hath **light
with darkness**?

2 Cor 6:14

21. He comes & goes on a cloud

And then shall they see the Son of man
coming in the clouds
with great power and glory.

Mark 13:26

And when he had spoken these things,
while they beheld,
he was taken up;
and **a cloud received him**
out of their sight.
And while they looked stedfastly **toward heaven
as he went up**, behold,
two men stood by them in white apparel;
Which also said,
Ye men of Galilee,
why stand ye gazing **up into heaven**?

This same Jesus,
>   which was **taken up** from you **into heaven**,
shall so come in like manner
>   as ye have seen him go **into heaven**.

Acts 1:9–11

22. Skull Place

Then Judas,
>   which had betrayed him,
>   when he saw that he was condemned,
>   repented himself,
>   and **brought** again the thirty pieces of silver
>   **to the chief priests and elders**.

Matt 27:3

And they bring him unto the place **Golgotha**,
>   which is, being interpreted,
>   The **Place of the Skull**.

Mark 15:22

And he bearing his cross
>   went forth into a place
>   called **the place of a skull**,
>   which is called in the Hebrew
>   Golgotha.

John 19:17

23. Crown of Thorns

And when they had platted a **crown of thorns**,
>   they put it upon his head,
>   and a reed in his right hand:
>   and they bowed the knee before him,
>   and mocked him, saying,
>   Hail, King of the Jews!

Matt 27:29

Then came Jesus forth,
>   wearing the **crown of thorns**,
>   and the purple robe.
And Pilate said unto them,
>   Behold the man!

John 19:5

24. Twelve Apostles

And when he called unto him his **twelve disciples**,
>   he gave them
>   power against unclean spirits, to cast them out,
>   and to heal all manner of sickness
>   and all manner of disease

Matt 10:1

And when the hour was come,
>   he sat down,
and the **twelve apostles** with him.

Luke 22:14

25. Trinity

(There are no biblical verses demonstrating or even supporting the Trinity concept. It is an unbiblical concept.)

26. In Temple at 12

And when he was **twelve years old**,

> they went up to Jerusalem after the custom of
> > the feast.

And it came to pass,

> that after three days they found him in the temple,
> sitting in the midst of the doctors,
> both hearing them and asking them questions.

Luke 2:42 & 46

27. Circle of the Seasons

> The **sun also ariseth**,
> > and the sun goeth down,
> > and hasteth **to his place where he arose** . . .
> The thing that hath been,
> > it is that which shall be;
> and that which is done
> > is that which shall be done:
> and there is **no new thing** under the sun .

Ecc 1:5, 9

28. Four Seasons

> And God said,
> > Let there be lights in the firmament of the heaven
> > to divide the day from the night; and
> > let them be for signs, and
> > for **seasons**, and
> > for days, and
> > years.

Gen 1:14

> He appointed the moon for **seasons**;
> > the sun knoweth his going down.

Ps 104:19

29. Circle of Sun / Calendar Dial / Born Again

> Is not God in the height of heaven?
> > and behold the height of the stars,
> > > how high they are
> And thou sayest,
> > What does God know?
> > Can he judge through the dark cloud?
> Thick clouds are a covering to him, that he seeth not;
> > and he walketh in the **circuit [or circle]** of heaven.

Job 22:12–14

It is he that sits above the **circle of the earth**,
> and the inhabitants thereof are as grasshoppers;

that stretcheth out the heavens as a curtain,
> and spreadeth them out **as a tabernacle**.

Isa 40:22

Except a man be **born again**,
> He cannot see the kingdom of God .

John 3:3

Marvel not that I said unto thee,
> Ye must be **born again**.

John 3:7

For as Jonas was **three days and three nights**
> in the whale's belly;

so shall the Son of man be **three days and three nights**
> in the heart of the earth.

Matt 12:40

And he began to teach them,
> that the son of man must suffer many things,
> and be rejected of the elders,
>> and of the chief priests,
>> and scribes,
> and be **killed**,
> and **after three days rise again**.

Mark 8:31, also 9:31

And said unto them,
> Thus it is written,
> and thus it behoved Christ to suffer,
> and to rise from the dead **the third day**.

Luke 24:46

30. Signs of the Zodiac

The heavens declare the glory of God
> and the firmament showeth his handiwork.

Day unto day **uttereth speech**,
> and night unto night **reveals knowledge**

There is no speech,
> there are no words,
> neither is their voice heard.

Their **line is gone out through all the earth**,
> and their words to the end of the world.

In them **he set a tabernacle for the sun**.
> which is as a bridegroom coming out of his chamber,
> and rejoices **as a strong man to run his course**.

His going forth is from the end of the heaven,
> and his **circuit [or circle]** unto the ends of it:

there is nothing hid from the heat thereof.

Psalm 19:1–6 (JPS)

Canst thou bring forth **Mazzaroth in his season**?
or canst thou **guide** Arcturus with his sons?

Job 38:32

31. Let Them Be "for Signs"

And God said,
>> Let there be lights in the firmament **of the heaven**
>>> to divide the day from the night;
>> and let them be
>>> for **signs**,
>>> and for seasons,
>>> and for days
>>> and for years.

Gen 1:14

The Pharisees also with the Sadducees came,
> and tempting desired him
that he would shew them
>> **a sign from heaven**.

Matt 16:1

And as he sat upon the Mount of Olives,
>> the disciples came unto him privately, saying,
>>> Tell us, when shall these things be?
>>> and what shall be **the sign** of thy coming,
>>> and of the end of the world?

Matt 24:3

Therefore the Lord himself shall give you **a sign**;
>> Behold a virgin shall conceive, and
>>> bear a son, and
>>> shall call his name Immanuel.

Isa 7:14

And there appeared **a great wonder [sign] in heaven**;
>> a woman clothed with the sun,
>> and the moon under her feet,
>> and upon her head a crown of twelve stars.
And there appeared another **wonder [sign] in heaven**;
>> and behold a great red dragon,
>> having seven heads,
>> and ten horns,
>> and seven crowns upon his heads.

Rev 12:1, 3

32. Passover & Death for 3 Days

For as Jonas was **three days and three nights**
> in the whale's belly;
so shall the Son of man be **three days and three nights**
> in the heart of the earth.

Matt 12:40

And he began to teach them,
    that the son of man must suffer many things,
    and be rejected of the elders,
        and of the chief priests,
        and scribes,
    and be **killed**,
    and **after three days rise again**.

Mark 8:31, also 9:31

And said unto them,
    Thus it is written,
    and thus it behoved Christ to suffer,
    and to rise from the dead **the third day**.

Luke 24:46

Then Moses called for all the elders of Israel,
    and said unto them,
Draw out and take you a lamb
    according to your families
    and **kill the passover**.

Ex 12:21

. . . therefore the Levites had the charge
    of the **killing of the passovers**
    for every one not clean,
    to sanctify them unto the Lord.

2 Chr 30:17

For even **Christ our Passover**
    is sacrificed for us .

1 Cor 5:7

33. Born of a Virgin

Therefore the Lord himself shall give you a sign;
Behold a virgin shall conceive, and
bear a son, and
shall call his name Immanuel.

Isa 7:14

And in the sixth month the angel Gabriel
    was sent from God unto a city of Galilee, . . .
To **a virgin** espoused to a man
    whose name was Joseph,
    of the house of David;
and **the virgin's name was Mary**.
And the angel came in unto her, and said,
    "Hail, thou that art highly favoured,
        the Lord is with thee:
    blessed art thou among women." . . .
And the angel said unto her,
    "Fear not, **Mary**:
        for thou hast found favour with God.
    And, behold, **thou shalt conceive** in thy womb,
        and **bring forth a son**,
        and shalt **call his name Jesus**."

Luke 1:26–31

34. Two Fishes

And they say unto him,
   We have here but five loaves, and **two fishes**.
And he commanded the multitude
    to sit down on the grass,
    and took the five loaves, and the **two fishes**,
    and looking up to heaven,
      he blessed,
and brake,
and gave the loaves to his disciples,
    and the disciples to the multitude.

Matt 14:17, 19

But he said unto them,
   Give ye them to eat.
And they said,
   We have no more but five loaves and **two fishes**;
   except we should go and buy meat for all this people.

Luke 9:13

There was a lad here,
   which hath five barley loaves,
   and **two small fishes**:
but what are they among so many?

John 6:9

35. Man with Water Pitcher

And he said unto them,
   Behold when ye are entered into the city,
   there shall **a man** meet you,
    bearing a pitcher of water;
   follow him into the house
    where he entereth in.

Luke 22:10

But whosoever drinketh of the water
   that I shall give him shall never thirst;
but **the water that I shall give him**
   shall be in him **a well of water springing up**
    into everlasting life.

John 4:14

He shall pour the **water out of his buckets**,
   and his seed shall be in **many waters**,
   and his king shall be higher than Agag,
   and his kingdom shall be exalted.

Num 24:7

36. In My Father's House

In my father's house are many mansions:
If it were not so,
   I would have told you.
I go to prepare a place for you.

John 14:2

37. End of the World

> The enemy that sowed them is the devil;
> the harvest is **the end of the world**;
> and the reapers are the angels.

Matt 13:39

> Teaching them to observe all things
>   whatsoever I have commanded you:
> and, lo, I am with you always
>   even unto **the end of the world**.
> Amen

Matt 28:20

38. Thirty Years Old

> . . . and Jesus himself began to be
>   about **thirty years of age** . . .

Isa 7:14

39. Walked on Water

> And in the fourth watch of the night
>   Jesus went unto them,
>   **walking on the sea**.

Matt 14:25–26

> So when they had rowed about
>   five and twenty or thirty furlongs,
> they see Jesus **walking on the sea**,
>   and drawing nigh unto the ship::
> and they were afraid.

John 6:19

40. Sun Calms the Sea

> And when he was entered into a ship,
>   his disciples followed him.
> And, behold, there arose a great tempest in the sea,
>   insomuch that the ship was covered with the waves:
>   but he was asleep.
> And his disciples came to him,
>   and awoke him, saying,
>   Lord, save us: we perish.
> And he saith unto them,
>   Why are ye fearful,
>   O ye of little faith?
> Then **he** arose,
>   and **rebuked the winds**
>   and **the sea**;
>   and **there was a great calm**.
> But the men marvelled, saying,
>   What manner of man is this,
>   that even the winds
>   and the sea obey him?

Matt 8:23–27

But as they sailed he fell asleep:
    and there came down a storm of wind on the lake;
    and they were filled with water,
    and were in jeopardy.
And they came to him, and awoke him, saying,
    Master, master, we perish.
Then **he** arose,
    and **rebuked the wind**
    and **the raging of the water**:
    and **they ceased**,
    and **there was a calm**.
And he said to them,
    Where is your faith?
And they being afraid wondered,
    saying one to another,
        What manner of man is this!
        for he commandeth
           even the winds
           and water,
    and they obey him.

Luke 8:23–25

41. King of Kings

Which in his times he shall shew,
    who is the blessed
        and only Potentate,
    the **King of kings**,
    and Lord of lords.

I Tim 6:15

And he hath on his vesture
and on his thigh a name written,
    King of kings,
    and Lord of lords.

Rev 19:16

42. 30 Pieces of Silver

And said unto them,
    What will you give me,
    and I will deliver him unto you?
And they covenanted with him
    for **thirty pieces of silver**.

Matt 26:15

Then Judas, which had betrayed him,
    when he saw that he was condemned,
    repented himself,
    and brought again the **thirty pieces of silver**
        to the chief priests and elders.

Matt 27:3

Then was fulfilled that
which was spoken
by Jeremiah the prophet, saying,
And they took the **thirty pieces of silver**,
the price of him that was valued,
whom they of the children of Israel did value?

Matt 27:9

43. Marriage Feast of Cana

And the third day
there was a **marriage in Cana** of Galilee,
and the mother of Jesus was there.
And both Jesus was called,
and his disciples, to the marriage.
When the ruler of the feast had tasted **the water
that was made wine**,
and knew not whence it was: . . .
But thou hast kept the good wine until now.
This the **beginning** of miracles
did Jesus **in Cana** of Galilee
and manifested forth his glory;
and his disciples believed on him.

John 2:1–11

44. Light of the World

As long as I am in the world,
I am the **light of the world**.

John 9:5

And art confident
that **thou thyself art** a guide of the blind,
a light of them which are **in darkness**.

Rom 2:19

45. The Word / Only Begotten

And **the Word** was made flesh,
and dwelt among us
(and we beheld his glory,
the glory as of the only begotten of the Father)
full of grace and truth

John 1:14

No man hath seen God at any time;
the **only begotten Son**,
which is in the bosom of the father,
he hath declared him.

John 1:18

In this was manifested
the love of God toward us,
because that God sent
his **only begotten Son** into the world,
that we might live through him.

I John 4:9

46. Born Again

See scriptual references 19 and 29.

47. The Sun with his Wings, Jesus

But unto you that fear my name
shall the **Sun of righteousness** arise
with healing **in his wings**;
and ye shall go forth,
and grow up as calves of the stall.

Mal 4:2

Oh Jerusalem, Jerusalem,
thou that killest the prophets, and
stonest them which are sent unto thee,
how often would I have gathered thy children together,
even as a hen gathereth her chickens **under her wings**,
and ye would not!

Matt 23:37, also Luke 13:34

48. Good Shepherd

I am the good shepherd:
the **good shepherd** giveth his life for the sheep
I am the good shepherd,
and I know my sheep,
and am known of mine.

John 10:11, 14

Now the God of peace,
that brought again from the dead our Lord Jesus,
that **great shepherd** of the sheep,
through the blood of the everlasting covenant.

John 10:11, 14

49. Rod and Staff

Yea, though I walk
through the valley of the shadow of death,
I will fear no evil:
for thou art with me;
thy rod and thy staff they comfort me.
Thou preparest a table before me
in the presence of mine enemies:
thou anointest my head with oil;
my cup runneth over.

Psalm 23:4–5

And she brought forth a man child,
who was to rule all nations
with a **rod of iron**:
and her child was caught up
unto God, and
to his throne.

Rev 12:5

And out of his mouth goeth a sharp sword,
that with it he should smite the nations:
and he shall rule them with a **rod of iron**:
and he treadeth the winepress of
the fierceness
and wrath of Almighty God.

Rev 19:15

50. Great Potter

But now, O Lord, thou art our father;
we are the clay and **thou our potter**; and
we all are the work of thy hand.

Isa 64:8

The word which came to Jeremiah from the Lord, saying,
"Arise, and go down to the **potter's house**,
and there I will cause thee to hear my words."
Then I went down to the potter's house, and,
behold, he wrought a work on the wheels.
And the vessel that he **made of clay**
was marred in the hand of **the potter**:
so he made it again another vessel,
as it seemed good to **the potter** to make it.
Then the word of the Lord came to me, saying,
"O house of Israel,
cannot I do with you as **this potter**?"
Saith the Lord.
"Behold, as **the clay is in the potter's hand**,
so are **ye in mine hand**,
O house of Israel. "

Jer 18:1–6

51. The Amen

For all the promises of God in him are yea,
and in him Amen,
unto the glory of God by us.

2 Cor 1:20

And unto the angel of the church of the Laodiceans write;
"These things saith the Amen,
the faithful and true witness,
the beginning of the creation of God."

Rev 3:14

52. Chief Cornerstone

And are built upon the foundation
of the apostles and prophets,
Jesus Christ himself being
the **chief cornerstone**.

Eph 2:20

Wherefore also it is contained in the scripture,
"Behold, I lay in Sion a **chief cornerstone**,
elect, precious:
and he that beliveth on him
shall not be confounded. 1

Pet 2:6

53. Ark of Noah

Too long to quote. See the text of Gen 6:14–8:22.

54. Manna from Heaven

And it came to pass,
that at even the quails came up,
and covered the camp:
and in the morning **the dew** lay round about the host.
And when the dew that lay was gone up, behold,
upon the face of the wilderness
there lay a small round thing,
as small as the hoar frost on the ground.
And when the children of Israel saw it,
they said one to another,
"**It is manna**": for they wist not what it was.
And Moses said unto them,
"This is the bread
which the Lord hath given you to eat."

Ex 16:13 15

55. Circumcision

This is my covenant, which ye shall keep,
between me and you
and thy seed after thee;
Every man child among you shall be circumcised.
And ye shall **circumcise** the flesh of your foreskin;
and it shall be a token of the covenant
betwixt me and you.

Gen 17:10–11

BIBLIOGRAPHY AND RECOMMENDED READING

1. *Origins of Religion* by Albert Churchward.

2. *Signs of Primordial Man* by Albert Churchward.

3. *Ancient Egypt: Light of the World* by Gerald Massey. (Available from The Book Tree)

4. *Book of the Beginnings* by Gerald Massey.

5. *Natural Genesis* by Gerald Massey.

6. *Lectures* by Gerald Massey.

7. *The Collected Works* of E. A. Wallis Budge

8. *Stellar Theology* by Robert Brown. (Available from The Book Tree)

9. *The Genesis of Christianity* by Prof. Hilton Hotema.

10. *Bible of Bibles* by Kersey Graves.

11. *Sixteen Crucified Saviors* by Kersey Graves. (Available from The Book Tree)

12. *Anacalypsis* by Godfrey Higgins. (Available from The Book Tree)

13. *Pagan Christs* by J. M. Robertson.

14. *Does Jesus Exist?* by G. A. Wells.

15. *Woman's Encyclopedia of Myths and Secrets* by Barbara Walker.

16. *Woman's Dictionary of Symbols* by Barbara Walker.

17. *Larousse Greek and Roman Myths*.

18. *Gospel In The Stars* by Joseph A. Seiss.

19. *Gospel of the Stars* by Peter Lemesurier.

20. *Secret Message in the Zodiac* by Troy Lawrence.

21. *Secret Teachings of all Ages* by Manly P. Hall.

22. *Astro-Theology* by Manly P. Hall.

23. *Occult Theocracy* by Edith Miller.

24. *Who Wrote the Bible?* by Richard Friedman.

25. *Mythology of all Races in Thirteen Volumes* by Archeological Institute of America.

26. *Folklore In the Old Testament* by Sir James G. Frazer.

27. *Serpent In the Sky* by John Anthony West.

28. *MacMillan Illustrated Encyclopedia of Myths and Legends* by Arthur Cotterell.

29. *Deceptions and Myths of the Bible* by Lloyd M. Graham.

30. *The Collected Works* of Zecharia Sitchin. (Available from The Book Tree)

31. *Myths of the World* by Padraic Colum.

32. *The Birth of Christianity* by Joel Carmichael.

33. *The collected Works* of Elaine Pagels.

34. *Complete series of Man, Myth and Magic*, occult encyclopedia.

35. *Pagans and Christians* by Robin Lane Fox.

36. *Jung and The Lost Gospels* by Stephan Hoeller.

37. *The Complete Works* of Max Muller.

38. *The Complete Works* of Joseph Campbell.

39. *A History of Religious Ideas* by Mircea Eliade.

DR. ALAN SNOW ON THE DEAD SEA SCROLLS
Interviewed by Jordan Maxwell

The discovery of the Dead Sea Scrolls beginning in 1947 was pivotal for a the study of the New Testament. One scholar who has kept current on all aspects of Dead Sea Scrolls studies and their impact on the New Testament, and biblical studies in general, is Dr. Alan Snow.

Dr. Snow obtained his Bachelor's Degree from Pepperdine University in 1969, his Master's Degree from the School of Theology, Claremont in 1974, and his Doctor of Theology degree from Andersonville Baptist Seminary in 1994. He has conducted special studies at the University of Judaism, Los Angeles (Jewish Theological Seminary of America) and at the Magister Operae Onerosae (hon.) from the Institute Antiquity Christianity, Claremont. Dr. Snow is a member of many professional organizations, including the Jesus Seminar. He is a contributing author to many books and articles on the subject of the Dead Sea Scrolls, origins of Christianity, and related biblical subjects. Astrologer Sidney Omar considers Dr. Snow the "World's greatest authority on astrology and the Dead Sea Scrolls."

Until recently, a large portion of the Dead Sea Scrolls material has been held back, available to only a few carefully selected scholars. The public release of the total corpus of the Dead Sea Scrolls material to scholars everywhere is expected to radically change current understanding of the New Testament, first century Judaism and the Roman world.

These changes in understanding will not bring comfort to orthodox Judaism, orthodox Christian denominations, or evangelical fundamentalism. In the following interview with Jordan Maxwell, Dr. Snow gives an excellent overview of the Dead Sea Scrolls and their significance to Judaism and Christianity of today and of the future.

JM: What are your thoughts on the Bible as a religious authority?

AS: I do not believe for a minute that there is any such thing as religious authority. I do not believe in the *Upanishads* as a religious authority. I do not believe in the Hebrew or Christian scriptures as a religious authority. I do not believe in the *Sutras* as a religious authority, or the *Koran.* So as far as the Bible is concerned as religious authority, to me it is literature that was created by men, for men. The Bible is a collection of many books often with inconsistent teachings, contradictory teachings, mythological teachings, folklore, some history, a lot of nonsense.

The Hebrew Language as Sacred

JM: The Hebrew language. We are given to understand in this country, in our religious institutions that the Hebrew language was that given to the human race by the Almighty God, the divine creator of the whole universe. It is a totally 100% accurate, absolute, exclusive language that no other human creature on the face of the earth has ever used but the divinely begotten ones of The Most High, who Himself who took time out from the creation of the great expanse of the universe to teach a handful of people the most holy of all holy languages that has ever existed on the face of the earth — and that is Hebrew. How do you feel about the language of Hebrew being the absolute most holy of all holy languages and the most divinely inspired language on the face of the earth?

AS: As the language of the Bible, the Hebrew language was used during the time of Solomon and after the time of Solomon. After the time of Solomon the books that we call "The Five Books of Moses": Genesis, Exodus, Leviticus, Numbers, and Deuteronomy, were put in writing. These stories, these legendary stories of Yahweh, were put in writing then. Later they were added to, cleaned up, some stuff dropped by what was called "redactors." Redactors are the later priestly revisers of the Bible.

So we are dealing with the Hebrew language that the priestly revisers spoke. No one knows the language that Abraham spoke; he may have been a mythological figure. Abraham, Ab-Ra-Am, father of nations, who knows what that means?

All the stories of Joseph, the stories of Moses, the stories even of David are considered to be the stories of Pharaohs' wars in that part of the world. The people of the Fertile Crescent, later called the Habiru, later the Hebrews, adopted the stories of Pharaoh, put David's name there, made the stories their own. So by the time you come to the successors of Solomon, at that time you are putting all that material in writing. Then that is later added to, subtracted from, elaborated.

You do not even have the book of Deuteronomy until much later after that. It was one of the kings of Judah (2 Kings 22–23) who supposedly went to the Temple and found the book of Deuteronomy. Where was it before? Well, it wasn't, that is the answer.

The language in the first five books of the Bible is the language that they were using at that time, after the time of Solomon, during the time of Rehoboam and that crowd.

One thing that the Dead Sea Scrolls have taught us was that there was no absolute canon of scripture as we understand it today. Even the language was changed. If the Essenes found something to be obscure in any of the Prophets or the books of Moses, they rewrote it. They wrote it in a language they could understand. That is why so much of the biblical sections of the Dead Sea Scrolls has not been published. It is because they do not agree with the Masoretic texts that have been handed down to us as the so-called, in your words, absolute words of Yahweh handed to Moses and the prophets and then handed to us unmolested for the last 4,000 years.

The Dead Sea Scrolls tell us that is not true and has never been true. You have in the Dead Sea Scrolls many families of the same scriptures. There are many families of the Torah, scriptural, textual families. You have the Palestinian family, you have the Babylonian family and you have various readings within these. Some of them are very old words. Some of them are very new words. That is why you have so much Aramaic thrown into the Old Testament sections that you find in the Dead Sea Scrolls. It is because they were speaking Aramaic. So they had to write the Scriptures in ways that they could understand.

In a few years this information will be published.

The Impact of the Dead Sea Scrolls Discovery

JM: How do you see the Dead Sea Scrolls affecting Judaism and Christianity, the religion of the Old and New Testament, once the entire story is finally out for public view and everyone, generally speaking, understands the bottom line on the Dead Sea Scrolls?

AS: So far the study of the Dead Sea Scrolls has not gone beyond the seminaries and universities. I go to all the lectures that are available to the general public, as well as professional lectures on the Dead Sea Scrolls. I am an alumnus, so I am informed when a scholar is going to speak on the Dead Sea Scrolls. I will go and listen. I do not think this will affect the general public — yet. That is because the general public simply does not read things that are as technical and as complicated as the Dead Sea Scrolls. Preachers do not preach about the Dead Sea Scrolls because their message is that what we were taught as fact, namely the New Testament and early church history as it has been handed down to us through our traditional mainstream churches, simply is not true.

The Dead Sea Scrolls are first-century documents that have not been revised, they have not been rewritten, they have come to us completely out of the blue. They are with us now and theologians at all the major seminaries that I attend, namely Hebrew Union College, the University of Judaism, the School of Theology at Claremont, their major studies in those schools have to do with interpreting the Dead Sea Scrolls, finding out where we have gone astray in our interpretation of first-century Judaism, Second Temple Judaism it is called. What the major theologians are doing right now is, they are rewriting early first-century Jewish and Christian history.

JM: That must impact the story of Christianity. It is going to have to impact our whole understanding of whether this story that we are reading in the New Testament was an actual legitimate, de jure, real-life story, or whether it was a metaphor, a spiritual, symbolic story. Right now, the church would have you believe that Christianity is the only single, legitimate theology on the face of the earth, the only one that is provable, the only one that is absolutely true. I am thinking when this whole story comes out, it is going to put into question the entire superstructure of Christianity.

AS: For scholars it already has. For Fundamentalists, it will not touch them at all. I have gone to lectures on the Dead Sea Scrolls presented by Fundamentalists, Catholics, and Mormon churches. Every lecturer there has misrepresented the Dead Sea Scrolls. They have said that the Dead Sea Scrolls confirm that what their churches teach is the truth. For someone like me who has read the Dead Sea Scrolls, to hear that is absolutely incredible.

Among the major scholars, first-century Judaism and Christianity have to be rewritten completely. In the Dead Sea Scrolls you have the first-century New Testament church being 200 years older than Jesus. You have a Nazarene movement, they call themselves Nozrei ha-Brit. They call themselves "Nazarenes" 200 years before Jesus. They had a system of communal poverty, or communal wealth depending on how you want to feel about it, shared wealth just as you find in the book of Acts. They were ruled over by bishops. They called the bishops *mabaker*. This is the Hebrew term for overseer. The word in Greek for overseer is *episkepos*. Our word for Episcopalian, for bishops, comes from the Greek. These are the overseers.

Two hundred years before we have the Christian church we have a religious Jewish community organized that is run by bishops sharing the wealth. They were baptizing themselves for remission of sins in what they called their *mikvahs*. (Today you have a *mikvah* in every Jewish synagogue where new converts are immersed in water, predominantly women. Convert men are circumcised or at least drawn blood if they are already circumcised.) You have a shared communal meal of bread and wine, which is considered a messianic meal. This is 200 years before the so-called Lord's Supper of Jesus where he breaks bread and gives out wine in this shared communion. This communion was common at that time among people who call themselves the Nazarenes.

Jesus was called "Jesus the Nazarene." In the New Testament it is pretty confused about how this term is used because you have Jesus being called Jesus of Nazareth, which archeologists now believe may or may not have been a little village outside of Sepphoris that was a major Greek town up near where Nazareth is now. The Sepphoris archeological digs are ongoing right now. There was a major Roman-Greek city 3 miles outside of the site of Nazareth. There is no place on any Roman map during the life of Jesus that is called Nazareth. But Jesus was called the Nazarene. By the time the New Testament writings were put together there was a Nazareth in that part of Judea and the Greek writers of the New Testament believed that maybe Jesus came from Nazareth

In all of Jewish history, including the time of Jesus, you were called after the place of your birth. He should have been called Jesus of Bethlehem. This is a major discussion going on in the Jesus Seminar. Jesus should have been called Jesus of

Bethlehem because that is where he was born, according to the text. But instead he is called Jesus of Nazareth. This is confusing because he is also called Jesus the Nazarene and "the Nazarenes" was the name of the Essenes. That is what they called themselves during the first century. They called themselves "the poor," "the Nazarenes," "the *Nozrei ha-Brit*," the keepers of the covenant. They had other names for themselves. *Osim* means something like healer. That is another term they would use. The Essenes is the term that is used by Josephus, Pliny the elder, and the other Roman historians at the time who were writing about the Essene movement.

The Essene headquarters was 15 miles outside of Jerusalem. These people were not secret. They were known everywhere throughout Judea at that time, according to the writings of Josephus. Yet in the New Testament you do not see the Essenes mentioned even once. But their language is there, all throughout the New Testament. From Matthew to Revelation. Revelation is filled with "Essenisms." The Book of Hebrews is filled with Essenisms. The Epistle of James could have been straight from the Qumran settlement 15 miles outside of Jerusalem. It is all this stuff about being zealous for the law, observing the Law of Moses, being faithful, righteous. All the language that you find throughout the Essene writings is there in certain of the Epistles.

Political Impact of the Dead Sea Scrolls

JM: What basically is going on in the State of Israel politically because of the Dead Sea Scrolls?

AS: The Jews are not concerned with the Dead Sea Scrolls at all. The Jewish religion that you have today is considered by scholars of the Dead Sea Scrolls to be one of the two permitted religions after the two failed revolts. The first revolt of 70 A.D. pretty much terminated the Qumran community and the Christian church in Jerusalem. Then there is the revolt of 134 A.D., that is, the revolt of Bar Kokhba. When that failed, all this stuff about eschatological religion, the study of the end-times, or the belief that they were living in the end-times, ended. Under Roman rule the rabbis agreed that they would give up this Essene eschatological-type thinking and they would be good little Roman Jews forever. They agreed to pray for the Roman emperor; they would live in the Roman empire they would love the Romans. They would be allowed, in return, to be one of the permitted religions in the Roman empire. The other permitted religion, tolerated to a point, was the Christians, up until the year 300 A.D. when they became the religion of the Roman empire. They were the two permitted religions in that part of the world at that time.

The Sadducees ended when the Temple was destroyed. The Essenes ended when their community headquarters 15 miles outside Jerusalem at Qumran was destroyed. That ended. Only the Pharisaic form of Judaism survived. That evolved into our Rabbinic Judaism. All of Judaism was then codified into the Mishnah and Gemara which is called the Talmud for us today. They built what the Essenes called "walls around their religion." That is what Judaism is today.

Judaism has absolutely no concern over the Dead Sea Scrolls. They could not care less. All the rabbis that I have ever talked to, all the Jewish scholars that I have ever talked to, even the ones that write the major books on the Essenes, agree, that the Dead Sea Scrolls do not concern Judaism. They are only of concern to Christianity.

JM: Even though the writers of the Dead Sea Scrolls were themselves Hebrew?

AS: They are not relevant to what Judaism is today. Judaism today is Rabbinic Judaism. They do not want to have anything to do with this kind of eschatological thinking, this kind of fundamentalism, this kind of narrow exclusive Judaism. At the time of Jesus there were many kinds of Judaism. Some were in opposition to each other. Josephus is filled with the wars of the Jews. These wars of the Jews are not just with outsiders: wars of the Jews were with each other. Very often the High Priest and his army would be against the Pharisees and their army. One would win and those who lost were put out on the street on crosses, hung from trees. Thousands of them. This is their own people being killed. These were wars within Judea, against each other, ideological wars, very important wars. The Jews today do not want to have anything to do with this Essene type of thinking because it has only been catastrophic to them in the past. They do not need it now.

JM: Is this the same kind of thinking that we are finding in the Christian Fundamentalist movement?

AS: Exactly. When you consider the Fundamentalists today, they have adopted what is called, in modern biblical scholarship, the Essene Hypothesis. That is the Essene doctrine of the "last days." The last days at the time of the Essenes in 70 A.D. They believed they were living in the last days then. They expected that when the Romans were coming in, Ezekiel was being fulfilled right then and there. Ezekiel 38–39. The Romans were there. They were in Ezekiel 38:11b and they were just about to get to Ezekiel 38:12a. They were living in the last days and they saw it happening. They got more and more fanatical, thinking that those were the last days. God, his angels and his saints would come and save them at the last minute.

It did not happen. It was catastrophic for Essene theology that the Romans won. That was not supposed to happen.

JM: What is the relationship between the Pharisees and the Essenes?

AS: Hostility. The Essenes referred to the Pharisees in the Dead Sea Scrolls as the "Builders of the Wall." They believed that the Pharisees were building too many laws around the Law. Their religion was too accommodating to the Romans. The Pharisees tried to get along with the Romans, they really did. So did the Herodian Sadducees.

But the fundamentalist Sadducees, the Essenes living out in Qumran, wanted an absolute fundamentalist, xenophobic (hate-foreigners) religion. They would be the head of it. The Essenes believed that in their lifetime they would see themselves, their organization, their leadership, as rulers in Israel. They believed that with the help of the angels and God, they would conquer the whole world, which would then come under the domination of their theology and their leaders.

I believe they almost saw this happen. When they were successful in 70 A.D. in capturing Jerusalem under the leadership of the Zealots — and remember, Zealots means being zealous for the Law. This is how the Essenes referred to themselves. They were zealous for the law. They were Zealots. When the Zealots captured Jerusalem they threw out Annas the High Priest, they killed him, they stoned him in the street. They threw out the Herodian priests whom they considered to be collaborators, Quislings, toadies of Herod and the Romans. And the Zealots put in their own priests.

Where did they get their priests? I believe the Zealots got their priests from the Essene community out there in Qumran. They all had pedigrees, they were all descendents of Aaron, they were all descendents of Zadok the High Priest. They claimed that they should be the rulers of the Temple in Jerusalem. I believe that for maybe about two years or less, the Essenes were able to have the High Priesthood in Jerusalem. This would also be part of their prophecy. This was part of their victory. This was one of the signs: that they were going to be victorious over the Romans and angels would then come and help them. It did not happen.

JM: That has shades of Zionism today?

AS: There are some Zionists who are this fanatical. My friend Dr. Jim Tabor, back in North Carolina, is in close contact with people who want to rebuild the Third Temple somewhere in Jerusalem. I have heard recently that there is a site of the Third Temple, maybe on the Mount of Olives or somewhere else. I say go for it. I think that would be fascinating. I would love to see that. I know that Dr. Tabor would also.

I think it is too long, too late. All of this should have happened in 70 A.D. We are 2,000 years away from this. It is a curiosity. I do not think it would mean a thing today. I think that most Jews would not care to have a Temple.

There are some Orthodox Jews who claim to have pedigrees going back to Aaron the High Priest. We call them the Cohenim. When I was attending temple during the times that I was studying Hebrew, I used to go every Friday night to the Jewish temple to keep up my Hebrew. They had the blessing of the priests. Anybody with the name of Cohen, Kahn, Caan, these men were considered to be priests of Israel. Whether they were or not, who cares, nobody cared. They would go up to the front of the synagogue and bless the congregation as the Cohenim of Israel. Where are they going to find the new Cohenim for the new Temple? Who knows? Maybe they have pedigrees going back to the time of the Babylonian captivity, fine.

I think that would be very interesting, but I think that most Jews today, who are Rabbinic Jews, do not care to have a Temple anymore. They have their synagogues. They have their traditions of the rabbis. Why reinstitute blood sacrifice? Blood sacrifice is not applicable today. Nobody cares any more. If they want to sacrifice, they will sacrifice prayers and make offerings to some charity. The Jews that I know have no interest in reinstituting the sacrifice of animals in a Temple in Israel.

JM: What is the real ideology behind this modern Zionist movement? Is someone trying to reestablish the religion of the ancient Hebrews as the dominant religion on the earth?

AS: As far as I know, from what I have read and known of Jews, the reason that they want a state is so they can be respected, have a state of their own and control their own holy places. In the last 2,000 years, the holy places of Judea and the Jewish religion have been in the hands of Christians and Moslems. Both Christians and Moslems are hostile to Jews. As far as they are concerned, Jews should not even exist. So the Christians and Moslems have been building their shrines on Jewish sites. The Christians have been erecting idols and temples on the Jewish sites. The Moslems have been building mosques. Both the Christians and the Moslems have been for the last 2,000 years carrying out pogroms and holy wars and crusades against the Jews, killing them as much as they can. So it is in the Jews' interest to have a state of their own so they can control their own destiny.

I have heard nothing in Zionism about rebuilding the Temple. I have not heard anything about their wanting to push the Moslems off the Temple Mount, although they could. Since 1967 they really could take over the Temple Mount, demolish the Mosque of Omar and begin rebuilding the Temple. Nobody. They have the arms, they can do it. That is the way it has always been in Judean history. Whoever has the most arms makes the laws.

When the Romans invaded in 130 A.D., they built a very nice city in Jerusalem. They called it Aelia Capitolina. They built a beautiful temple on the Temple Mount in honor of the Roman god Jupiter. They built shrines throughout the city of Jerusalem honoring all the gods and goddesses of Rome and the emperors. They had the army, they did it.

They built a Roman city on the ruins of Jewish Jerusalem. And they built it like any Roman city anywhere in the Roman empire. On the Temple Mount they built a temple to Jupiter and had sacrifices there to Jupiter. After the revolt ended in 135 A.D., the Jews could not come into that city any more. They built Roman baths, they built temples, anything that a normal Roman city would have, they built. Only citizens who were loyal to Rome could live there.

JM: Who built it?

AS: Aelia Capitolina was the name of the Roman city that was planted on top of the ruins of Jerusalem. They renamed the city. The Romans dropped the name Jerusalem and named it Aelia Capitolina.

JM: The person, the man Jesus, the one Christians think of when we talk about Christianity and the Bible in the New Testament. What are your feelings about the person or the man?

AS: My personal feeling is that he is totally fictitious. He is a remake of Serapis of Egypt. But from a Dead Sea Scrolls point of view and the view of many scholars in this field, James the Just is a spitting image of what Jesus was. James the Just replaced Jesus. James the Just was the brother of Jesus. When Jesus was dead and buried, James the Just replaced him as the head of the proto-Christian-Jewish community in Jerusalem. The church at that time was ruled by the three pillars, Peter, James the Just, and John. They were part of the Council of Twelve, which was the same kind of setup that Qumran had 15 miles outside of Jerusalem. They were ruled over by 3 priests and 12 laymen who were members of the Council of Twelve who ruled over the Essene community. According to modern scholarship, that includes the Dead Sea Scrolls. Whatever James was, Jesus was. Whatever Jesus was, James was. James is the only real proof that there was an historical Jesus.

JM: Okay. When you say that, the man James the Just would have been a prototype of the one we would call Jesus?

AS: He was his successor.

JM: The one we call Jesus, would that have been the Jesus that is in the Bible?

AS: No. That New Testament Jesus is a total fiction. Most of what Jesus is believed to have said is now known to have been put in his mouth by later writers one to two hundred to three hundred years later, especially the stuff that is anti-Jewish, which has to have been put in by an anti-Jewish writer two hundred years after Jesus.

All this stuff about love the prostitutes, pay your taxes, follow the centurion for two miles, respect Rome, pray for the emperor, give up Torah, do not observe the Sabbath, circumcision is not important. All of these things are the exact opposite of what James the Just and the early church taught in the New Testament itself. What we have today in Christianity is the Gentile-ized religion of Paul, who is now believed, in the light of the Dead Sea Scrolls, to have been a Herodian collaborator. Paul was a close associate of Herod, Herod's court. Many of his friends were Herodians. Many of his friends were Romans. He claimed Roman citizenship, Roman loyalty. He did everything he could to promote a Herodian-style, universal religion for the empire that included some elements of Judaism but a lot of the universalism of the Roman empire from the time of Constantine to today as the Christian religion.

JM: Paul performed the same act for the religion of Judaism as Josephus did for the history of Judaism of the time?

AS: Yes. Josephus wrote as a friend of Rome. When referring to Jewish rebels (during the time of the revolt, he would have called them freedom fighters), Josephus called them thieves and murderers. It is all a matter of interpretation. If the Jewish revolt had been successful, they would have been writing the history of the Jewish revolt and it would have been written in the style of the Maccabees. You would have had heroes and everybody would love them and they would have been victorious and we would be celebrating their feast days. But they lost, so now they are called thieves, murderers, *Sicarii*, and assassins. What they were for themselves and for their people, at that time, they were freedom fighters against Roman tyranny. They lost. They did not write the history. The Romans did, through Josephus.

JM: The Holy Days of the Hebrews, that we are given to understand are very, very holy, given by the most high sovereign god, what is some background of what we call the Hebrew Holy Days?

AS: They are the feast days that you find in the Old Testament. The Succoth is the Feast of Tabernacles, the Passover celebrates the coming out of Egypt, the Firstfruits is something the Essenes came up with, They are the normal holidays that any tribal religion would have at that time. The Feast of Purim was celebrating the victory of the Jews in Iran, in Persia at that time under Queen Esther; they were able to save themselves.

JM: What I was getting to is that I have gone through many reference books in the Hebrew libraries that basically say that all of these holidays are agricultural or seasonal, which were later on given the stories about the Maccabees and whatever. But in point of fact they were already well in existence a long time ago, before any angels or before any holiness was ever attributed to them and that they were seasonal. They celebrated the planting and gathering of food.

AS: That would make sense. I am sure if we ever got to know the seasonal feasts of the Babylonians, the Assyrians, Phoenicians and Egyptians, we would find that they paralleled what the Jews were doing.

JM: That is exactly what the reference works were saying. The thing that has so bothered me for so many years is that in the Western world, especially in America, we have been given to understand that the Hebrew God is the actual sovereign single, only divine creator of the whole universe and that nothing else in this entire world and spectrum of the human race is of any value or any importance. Only that divine one of Israel is the Almighty. Where did this Hebrew religion, where did this Hebrew people actually originate? Is all of this directed from the almighty, divine, heavenly Father, or is this merely one Hebrew religion, one facet of a great Semitic story in the ancient world?

AS: Up until about 100 years ago, that would have been the view. That would have been the only view you would have had of the Hebrew religion. One God, one religion, passed down to us unchanged. Since then I have been to many lectures at Hebrew Union College and the University of Judaism and I have never heard a rabbi say that. All the rabbis that I know of, but I never heard an orthodox rabbi speak. I do not go to orthodox seminaries. I never heard a modern, educated rabbi who did not fully admit that God, and the names of God, came from the deities that were popular in ancient Judea at the time of David and Solomon. What they did is, they combined these many gods that were the gods of the mountain and the gods of the volcanoes and the gods of the valleys — the "Els," the "Elohim," the "Yahwehs," the "Ashera" who was the wife of Yahweh well, they dropped her later. These names of God were all names of deities and rocks that were popular at that time. They were all brought together into one amalgamation of one God with all these ancient names, each of which has a history of its own, and they do not question it today. "El-ha-Shadai" is what, Lord of the Mountain.

I recently went to a lecture two weeks ago at the University of Judaism where the speaker was talking about the different bulls that were dug up and used in the shrines. All of these bulls were the "Els" of the cities. They were all called "El."

JM: Is there any hint of idolatry or paganism in the Dead Sea Scrolls?

AS: In the sectarian material, no. This is because you are dealing with Jewish fundamentalists. They were very, very "anti-" any form of paganism. The only mention of idolatry that you have in the Dead Sea Scrolls is in the canonical scriptures, namely Leviticus, Deuteronomy and the condemnation of idolatry that you would find in the Prophets. Those you may also consider to be Dead Sea Scrolls because every biblical book of the Old Testament has been found in the Qumran corpus except the book of Esther.

JM: How does this compare to idolatry or paganism in the churches of today? Is it similar or different?

AS: Since they did not have any kind of statues or sacred stones or anything like that in the Dead Sea Scrolls, or in any of the archeological digs, then there is no comparison at all. Modern Christianity is filled with symbolisms, statues, icons. What you have in modern Christianity is a combination of monotheism and the pagan religion and symbols of Rome and Greece.

The Documents within the Dead Sea Scrolls

JM: Can you give us a short list of the major documents of the Dead Sea Scrolls?

AS: Yes. Of course, it is no longer a short list. You have over 800 different manuscripts represented in the Dead Sea Scrolls. But I can give you some idea.

First of all you have the canonical scriptures. I mentioned that already. You have the sectarian material which you call the Community Rule or the Damascus Document. Both of those describe the order of the Essenes and how they live and why they are there.

You have the War Rule, which is called the War Scroll. That is the tentative plan, the battle plan for the end of the world. You have the Temple Scroll which describes how the new temple, the ideal temple, would be built, how many feet this way and that way, and what was to be in it, and so on. Their temple is quite nice.

You have lots of hymns, liturgies, and what is called Wisdom Poetry. This is very much like reading the book of Psalms and the book of Proverbs, the wisdom literature. They have lots of lamentations, Words of the Heavenly Light, songs for the Holocaust of the Sabbath, liturgical prayers, daily prayers, blessings, Triumph of Righteousness. These are just some of the kind of scrolls that you will find in the liturgical section.

You have the bible interpretations, the commentaries, on the biblical sections where they interpret places like the Old Testament books of Habakkuk, Nahum, Micah, commentaries on Hosca, commentaries on the Psalms. They really make the Old Testament come alive for them, for where they are in the first century. They really believed they were living in the "last days," so they interpreted the Old Testament writings as referring to them as the remnant in the "last days."

JM: They made direct application to their time?

AS: Oh definitely. They thought that the Prophets were writing about them. In other words, just like modern Christian Fundamentalists today believe that the Prophets are writing about us today. The Prophets were writing about the Anti-Christ, about the Tribulation, about the "last days," about the chosen remnant, about the falling away, and all that stuff. They believed that just as the Fundamentalists today believe that they are living in the "last days" and the Bible is as alive to them today as the daily newspaper, that was the way it was for the Essenes in the first century.

In addition to the biblical interpretations they also have what Bible scholars call "Miscellanea." This is material that the modern biblical scholars would rather not deal with, but it is there anyway in the Dead Sea Scrolls, namely the astrological sections and the horoscopes, the section called Brontologion (4Q318), which means "thunder words." It has to do with mystical interpretations to the thunder when it is heard over the community. They think that had meaning to them.

Then, of course, you have the mysterious Copper Scroll. You have every imaginable interpretation today of the Copper Scroll. For one, it was a fraud, just a fiction thrown in there to confuse people. Or maybe it was a guide to the Herodian Temple treasury that was buried throughout Judea in secret places that were recorded in the Copper Scroll so that after the war when the priesthood and the Temple was functioning again, their surrogates could go out to these areas and bring back the treasury of the Temple. And then I heard a new theory just yesterday from one of your friends, Jordan, that the Copper Scroll is a Babylonian mystical guide done in symbols that shows where the Temple treasury is. This concept sounds interesting.

So that is in a nutshell what the corpus of the Dead Sea Scrolls are.

JM: The Manual of Discipline is the Damascus Scroll?

AS: The Damascus Document, the Manual of Discipline, what you have there are various names for the same thing: the Community Rule, the Damascus Document, the Manual of Discipline. What you have is that the early translators of the Scrolls called it the Manual of Discipline because it was similar to the Methodists' organizational document, also called the Manual of Discipline.

The Damascus Document is very similar. Both of these documents are organizational documents. They say who is running the show, one mentions the Teacher of Righteousness, the other does not. So one is probably earlier than the other. The Damascus document and the Manual of Discipline were both attempts to provide structure for religious orders. The rules of the Catholic Benedictine Order were about how to conduct ceremonies, who gets in, and they outline what happens to you when you commit certain kinds of ritually unacceptable sins or transgressions of the rules. For example, if you spit to the left or the right, one is correct and one is incorrect, and you are punished for that transgression. Or if you speak out of turn in an assembly, you will be silenced for six months.

It is this kind of material in the Damascus Document and the Manual of Discipline. They read almost like a Catholic catechism. If you do this, you say five Our Fathers; if you do that, you say ten Hail Marys. Both of those documents are very picky and detailed and hairsplitting.

JM: The Thanksgiving Scroll?

AS: The Thanksgiving Scroll is a name that was arbitrarily given to their book of hymns. When you read through them, remember that the name "Thanksgiving Scroll" is again based on Christian thinking. It is a very nice way to describe this kind of poetry. I have read them all. They read like the Psalms of David, but they are more sectarian than our hundred and fifty Psalms. The Thanksgiving Hymns are extremely self-centered and very anti-foreigner and very anti-anybody who does not keep the law of Moses. They curse unbelievers. They curse Jews who have betrayed the law of Moses. They are pretty negative, but they are interesting. They are the kind of hymns and songs and poetry that you would expect from an extremist sectarian group that was very self-righteous.

JM: In other words, "Thank you Lord for not making me like 'them,'" and thank you for letting me bash the brains out of my enemies."

AS: That would be very typical of what you read in the Thanksgiving hymns. They express what they believe about themselves.

The Dead Sea Scrolls and the Bible

JM: How close are the biblical Scrolls to the Masoretic Text?

AS: Close enough so that if you wanted to be comfortable with the King James Version, Douai-Reims Version, New World Translation Version, you would be all right with the 39 books of the Old Testament. You could live with that. For someone who wants to study in detail, you have enough differences to keep you busy. The differences are not that major also, unless you are a biblical fundamentalist. You have certain of the Hebrew scrolls at Qumran that parallel what is called the Egyptian family tradition, which would be the Septuagint. You have enough differences in the Qumran Old Testament Scrolls so that they parallel what is called the Samaritan family tradition. They have that kind of wording. Then you have the proto-Masoretic rabbinic texts. Those are there also. After the Qumran community was terminated by the Romans in 70 A.D. the only surviving group that was allowed to exist by the Romans is the Pharisaic group from which all Judaism is descended, the Rabbinic tradition. They are the ones at Yavne around 100 A.D. who decided to codify Judaism and to canonize the biblical books in a way that would be uniform throughout Judaism. They are the ones who decided on the Masoretic text and decided to drop the Samaritan and Egyptian traditions.

JM: Are any of the biblical books in Hebrew only?

AS: Hebrew and Aramaic, yes. However, in Cave 7 you have the Greek Septuagint manuscripts of the Old Testament. In Cave 7 — and this is open to dispute, but it seems as if there is a lot there in evidence of this theory — that certain New Testament texts have been found in Cave 7, very detailed texts. Enough fragments have been found that fit exactly certain parts of the New Testament books of Peter, certain parts of Mark, just as they fit certain other parts of the Old Testament word for word. In fact, the correspondence is so close that I can see them being there. They are parts of the words of things: he walked, Lake of Gennesaret, loaves and fishes, things that totally fit in with the Gospel story.

JM: So a person could take those fragments two ways, one being that the Gospel books were written early and found their way there, the other being that they originated from the Dead Sea community?

AS: There is enough lack of information, lack of dates, lack of names on the Scrolls so that there is room for a huge amount of speculation about when the Gospels and the Epistles were written. Remember none of that literature is dated by the other. It does not say "I, Paul in the 5th year of Nero wrote this book in Antioch." It would be very nice if they did date and sign their works, but they did not. None of the Dead Sea Scrolls have dates on them. So you have people like Robert Eisenman and Barbara Thiering and other scholars who are dating these materials very, very early, 200 B.C., or they are dating them as late as 60–65 A.D. There is room for argument on both sides, which is what makes this subject so interesting.

JM: Over what period of time is it thought the Dead Sea Scrolls were written?

AS: The Dead Sea Scrolls were written from 200 B.C., about, to 70 A.D. I have heard from some scholars that it is possible that some of these caves had scrolls put in them as late as 135 A.D., which would have been the second Jewish revolt against Rome. Remember, you are dealing with predominantly biblical style material. These are not historical records that tell the history of their times in detail. They do not write about the Teacher of Righteousness and who he was and what year he came there. You have very general type information here that makes it impossible to date. So this material could go as late as 135 A.D., but the great majority consensus scholarship believes it ended in 70 A.D.

JM: Other dating methods like carbon dating do not help us in this case?

AS: Not much. Carbon dating has been difficult for everything at that time period, because carbon dating allows 100 years plus or minus from the date indicated. When you are trying to pinpoint it down to a ten-year span, carbon dating is not helpful. The material is definitely first century. Nobody doubts that. There were some speculations by a few scholars that the Dead Sea Scrolls were medieval forgeries. I do not know of anybody who believes that today. Every credible biblical scholar places them in the first century.

JM: Earlier you mentioned astrology. Did the Dead Sea Scrolls community have their own calendar system?

AS: They had a calendar system that was a solar calendar system, as opposed to the lunar calendar system that was being used by the Herodian Sadducees in Jerusalem. It threw them off by a day but it was not a very important difference for my studies.

They were astrologers. They believed in the signs of the times. They believed that the skies told the future. They did watch the stars and the planets and they did record horoscopes. These were found in the Dead Sea Scrolls.

JM: Did they keep Passover at a different time?

AS: I believe they did because if you notice in the Gospel of John, as opposed to the other three Gospels, you have a different timing there of when Jesus celebrated the Passover. It is very possible that John is talking about the Essene calendar as opposed to the calendar being used in Jerusalem. In the Dead Sea Scrolls the Teacher of Righteousness was killed or wounded by the Wicked High Priest who came to his encampment, which was not far from Jerusalem — I keep repeating this to people, it is only fifteen miles outside of Jerusalem. The High Priest came on a normal day for the High Priest's calendar, but it was a holy day for the Essenes. So they were keeping a different calendar and it was a Sabbath for the Essenes and it was not one for the Wicked Priest. That had always been a bone of contention between the Essene Sadducees, which is what Lawrence Schiffman would like to call them, as opposed to the Herodian Sadducees who followed the lunar calendar in Jerusalem.

The Teacher of Righteousness

JM: Tell us about the Teacher of Righteousness.

AS: He is a totally mysterious figure. Many scholars believe that he was dissident Zadokite priest who may have been one of the deposed High Priests of Jerusalem when the Hasmoneans took over the government of Judea. He may have been a lone figure.

Then again, the title Teacher of Righteousness may have been one that was handed down. You may have had one Teacher of Righteousness after another. This is what Robert Eisenman believes. He believes that James the Just, the brother of Jesus, was a Teacher of Righteousness a *sadek moray*, which means "right teacher," "correct teacher," and that he was the head of the community of the Jerusalem early proto-Christians who were totally Jewish. They went to the Temple every day, observed Sabbath, circumcision, the Holy Days of Jewish people, and had very little to do with Gentiles, as opposed to Paul, who is now considered by many scholars to be a Herodian worker trying to found a new universal religion that would include Judaism and paganism in the laissez-faire of the Roman Empire. Do away with Torah, do away with observing the Law, circumcision, all these things that divided Jews from non-Jews.

JM: Is the Teacher of Righteousness thought to be the chief author of the commentaries?

AS: He is believed to have authored many of the psalms that are in the Dead Sea Scrolls, the so-called Thanksgiving Hymns. He may or may not have written the Damascus Document or the Community Rule. That could have been put together by committee or it could have been written by him, or at least with him as the inspiration.

It is believed that the Teacher of Righteousness may have written the document called the "MMT." This document has been an extremely controversial document. It is a letter written by the head of the Qumran community, most likely the Teacher of Righteousness, to his opposite head, the leader of the Children of Israel, whoever he was, whether he was the High Priest, or King Herod, or who knows — nobody knows because it's not clear in the document. In that letter, believed to be written by the Teacher of Righteousness, to his opposite head in Jerusalem, is outlined the differences between the Temple Herodian establishment in Jerusalem and the dissident Sadducean Essene establishment fifteen miles outside of Jerusalem in the Qumran area. They were upset over the offering of prayers for the Emperor, they were upset over Gentiles being allowed to bring offerings. They felt that made the Temple unclean. They were upset over the kind of animals that were being offered in the Temple. They did a lot of hair-splitting over things like whether water was pure for cleansing. It had to be flowing water as opposed to still water. All these hair-splitting things, very important to the Essenes, apparently were not so crucial to the Herodian Sadducees who were running the show in Jerusalem in the first century.

JM: You mentioned briefly the historical identification of the Teacher of Righteousness. What are the different theories as to who he was?

AS: The Teacher of Righteousness could have been an early dissident High Priest who was dethroned or fired by one of the Hasmonean kings. He may have gone out into the desert with a group of followers where he would be there as opposition High Priest with his opposition group of holier-than-thou Temple assistants, many of whom were also descendants of the Son of Zadok which would make them priests, Cohenim. People who claimed to have the right to be the priests of the Temple as opposed to the ones who were there who were being appointed by foreign rulers, whether it was a Greek, a Syrian, a Roman ruler, or a Herodian prince who was appointed by Rome — either way the Sadducean priests of Jerusalem were being appointed by foreign rulers and were basically puppets of foreign rulers.

The Essenes out in the desert believed that they were the pure ones and they wanted to overthrow, or at least get the foreign rulers out of Israel. It seems to be an impossible thing, rather ridiculous at the time. They certainly did not have the power of the army to do it. But this is what they wanted to do.

JM: Were there not other theories that the Teacher of Righteousness was John the Baptist?

AS: Yes. You have the various theories of Eisenman and Thiering and then the mainstream establishment scholarship of the École Biblique. Eisenman believes that the Teacher of Righteousness was a very late teacher, namely James the Just, the brother of Jesus. This is because in the *Clementine Chronicles* that Eisenman refers to and Josephus mentions, James the Just fits the prototype of the Teacher of Righteousness in the Scrolls. Annas, the last High Priest before the Romans were kicked out in the first revolt, fit the prototype of the High Priest. Annas was a very unjust High Priest, taxing and vexing the people. He forced them to pay their due to the Temple, beat them up, and so on. Then you have Barbara Thiering who believes John the Baptist was the Teacher of Righteousness and Jesus was the Wicked High Priest, or the Man of Sin.

You also had a St. Paul-type person who was called the Man of Lies. When you read the Pauline Epistles he's constantly saying, I'm not lying and so on. It may be that Eisenman is right, that Paul is the Man of Lies. We know that the Gospel was for the Gentiles. It was abhorrent to the Jerusalem establishment under James the Just, who was one of the three pillars running the proto-Christian church, the Jewish Christians in Jerusalem. They were called the three pillars: Peter, James and John were ruling over the council of twelve apostles. They were all Jewish at that time.

All went to the Temple. All believed in observing the Law of Moses. It mentions in the book of Acts that they were zealous for the Law. They would have been very good Jews at that time.

JM: How certain is it that the Teacher of Righteousness was a priest? James the brother of Jesus was not a priest.

AS: That is true. That is where this mythology of being a priest according to the order of Melchizedek comes in the book of Hebrews. Then in the Dead Sea Scrolls, many sections mention the mysterious Melchizedek. He is almost a magical figure in the Dead Sea Scrolls. So you have a connection there between being a priest according to the order of Melchizedek.

In the Dead Sea Scrolls you have a Messiah of David and a Messiah of Aaron. The authors of the Dead Sea Scrolls expected two Messiahs. It is possible that Jesus could have been the expected dynastic claimant for the Messiah of David. It is possible that his cousin John the Baptist was considered a candidate to be the Messiah of Aaron. Remember that John the Baptist's father was one of the priests operating in the Temple at that time. John the Baptist's mother was, according to the biblical text, the cousin of Mary, the mother of Jesus. So you have in the same family a branch of David and a branch of Aaron. It is another feather in the cap of Robert Eisenman that there is this connection, this possibility. It fits the scenario of the Dead Sea Scrolls.

Another thing, when Jesus died, he was succeeded as head of the Jerusalem community by James the brother of the Lord. When James was killed later on, around the late 60s A.D, just before the Jewish revolt, he was succeeded by one of the nephews of Jesus named, I believe, Simon. You are dealing with a family dynasty where blood relatives were succeeding each other as head of the Jewish community in Jerusalem which may well have been the Essene community.

They were using the same kind of language for themselves that you find in the New Testament. They refer to themselves as *Nozrei ha-Brit*, the Nazarenes. They referred to themselves as "the poor," the people of the poor. The poor are referred to throughout the New Testament and the Dead Sea Scroll material. They referred to themselves as "the many." Remember in the Epistles it is the many this, the many that. That is the way they would talk about themselves in the Damascus Document and the Community Rule. They referred to the many this, when the many gathered. It is called *Harabim*.

So you have this huge similarity in language between the Essene community and the early Jerusalem Church that you just cannot get around. The fact that in the New Testament you never once have any mention of the Essenes. Even though they are a prominent group at that time in Judea, you never see them mentioned. Many scholars believe that they are not mentioned in the New Testament writings because the New Testament writings are the Essene writings. They were written by them.

You have so many parallels between the New Testament and the Dead Sea Scrolls. You have beatitudes. We are all familiar with the beatitudes of Jesus. A lot of people do not know about the beatitudes that are in the Dead Sea Scrolls. I will read three lines, to give you a sample:

> Blessed is [blank] with a pure heart,
> and does not slander with his tongue.
> Blessed are those who hold to her wisdom's precepts,
> and do not hold to the ways of iniquity.
> Blessed are those who rejoice in her
> and do not burst forth in ways of folly.

So you have a similarity in language that they were using. The Dead Sea Scrolls community had the laying-on of hands as was practiced in the New Testament. In the Genesis Apocryphon of the Dead Sea Scrolls you have this one verse that stands out:

> So I prayed for him and I laid my hands on his head
> and the scourge departed from him
> and the evil spirit was expelled from him,
> and he lived.

You had the laying-on of hands for healing which was a common practice in the New Testament community. In the section of the Dead Sea Scrolls called the Aramaic Apocalypse, you have this very strange phrase,

> The Son of God, he will be proclaimed,
> and the Son of the Most High they will call him.

This is an amazing kind of language. In traditional Christianity that phrase was used exclusively of Jesus. But in the Dead Sea Scrolls it refers to the King of Israel. That seems to be the normal kind of language.

In the New Testament they talked about individuals being the Temple. "Destroy this temple and in three days I will raise it up." In the Dead Sea Scrolls you have this midrash on the last days. You have this unusual expression saying,

> He has commanded that a sanctuary of men
> be built for Himself;
> That there may be sent up like the smoke of incense
> the works of the Law.

So they considered themselves a spiritual Temple out in the desert. That is extremely unusual language for that time. And it is typical of the New Testament.

I would also like to mention the communion service that the Essenes had. It has always been thought that Jesus and his disciples were unique with the service of bread and wine that he had at the Last Supper. Listen to how the Dead Sea Scrolls community celebrated a messianic supper. This was a common supper. It might have been celebrated once a week, it might have been celebrated every day. It can be found in the Messianic Rule in the Scrolls. It says,

> And when they shall gather for the common table
> to eat and to drink new wine;
> When the common table shall be set for eating
> and the new wine poured for drinking;
> Let no man extend his hand over the firstfruits of bread
> and wine before the priest.
> For it is he who shall bless the firstfruits of bread and wine
> and shall be the first to extend his hand over the bread.
> Therefore, the Messiah of Israel shall extend his hand
> over the bread;
> and all the congregation shall utter a blessing,
> each man in the order of his dignity.
> It is according to this statute that they shall proceed at
> every meal where at least ten men are gathered together.

Listen to that. Does it not sound a lot like holy communion? "They shall proceed at every meal at which at least 10 men are gathered together." And this was in the Messianic rule. This was a service of bread and wine celebrated in the name of the Messiah. Does it not sound a lot like the holy communion that is celebrated in every Protestant, Catholic and Eastern Orthodox church throughout the world? The comparisons are incredible.

The Messiah in the Dead Sea Scrolls

JM: Did they consider the Messiah to be divine or merely a man sent from God to save the people physically?

AS: All the messiahs that are spoken about in the Scriptures, in the Dead Sea Scrolls, and in the Old Testament, have been mortals and not all messiahs — you know, every king of Israel is a messiah. All the word means is "anointed one." All the High Priests of Israel have been messiahs. They were all anointed. They were all "anointed of the Lord."

Not only that, remember, even Cyrus the Great, a pagan, was considered a messiah. So the word "messiah" can be used in many, many ways. The word "messiah" refers to men, not to gods, not to divine beings, not to angels. All the messiahs are men who will die. They are not divine, they are just "anointed of the Lord" and they will be succeeded by other messiahs.

What happens after the coming of the great messiah that they talk about, the new age? See, the Essenes believed that a new age was coming in which Judaism and their interpretation of what Israel was to be, would be supreme throughout the whole world. If that is kind of an immortality for them, if they would live forever, I do not know. It is not exactly clear in the Dead Sea Scrolls. You can take a choice on that.

JM: Is it fair to say that Judaism today is a "Roman approved" Judaism without a messiah?

AS: Yes. Definitely. It is considered one of the permitted faiths. It is one of the permitted faiths that were allowed by Rome to survive. The other two forms of Judaism, called philosophies by Josephus, were not allowed to survive. The Sadducees did not survive and could not survive without the Temple. There is no use to the Jewish community to have Sadducees supported by the community if there is no Temple for them to work in.

You do have today nice guys who are named Cohen who are treated every now and then at public services every Friday night as Cohenim [priests] and they do give a priestly blessing to the community. I have seen this many times. They are not paid to do this. They are just one of many Jews who attend Sabbath services.

The other groups of Jews who were not allowed to survive by Rome are the Sicarii or the Zealots, the revolutionaries. The Essenes, when their prophecies failed, must have been very discouraged. They must have been more discouraged than any Jehovah's Witness, or Mormon, or Seventh Day Adventist that we have read about in church history who thought that Jesus was going to come back in 1844, and then they pushed it ahead to 1914. It did not matter. After the prophecies begin to fail, people lose heart and they begin to make other decisions.

It is believed that after the war of 70 A.D. when the Essenes were completely defeated along with the nation of Judea, many of them became what was called the Ebionites, which were called the "poor ones." The "poor ones," that is an Essene term. It is believed that many of the Essenes joined the early Christian church. It says in the book of Acts that in that day many of the priests joined the congregation (Acts 6:7). It is believed now that, considering the similarity in language between the Dead Sea Scrolls and the New Testament language, that was an expression for the Essenes. The priests joined the community. That would make sense.

What happened to them after that? I think many were killed, many were sold into slavery, many lost faith and just became good Jews living in whatever reservations that were set aside for them by the Romans like Yavne. That's what happened to them afterwards.

JM: James the brother of Jesus, was he an historical figure?

AS: James the brother of Jesus is mentioned in a lot of the early Christian literature as a Jewish figure. He is historically correct for the time. He does not have a lot of the paganized mythology around him that is later thrown around Jesus and the apostles. He is mentioned by Josephus. That may have been a later addition, but a lot of scholars believe that Josephus truly did write about James being killed by a mob of Herodians. Historically I personally believe that James fits in with first-century Judaism. I agree with Robert Eisenman when he says that James is the proof that there was an historical Jesus. What James was, Jesus was. And what Jesus was, James was.

JM: That could be understood two separate ways. Because James was an actual historical figure, then that means he had a brother named Jesus?

AS: Yes. That could be true.

JM: Or, I am saying that because James actually existed, he was the one that the mythical Jesus would have been patterned on?

AS: There is also room for that. That would be a great Ph.D. thesis. You could say that. The historical Jesus, if there is such a thing, and the Jesus Seminar is researching this in great detail. If there was such a thing as an historical Jesus, he has been so mythologized in the New Testament and by the later Constantinian church, that we cannot possibly know who or what Jesus was. It is impossible.

Based on the information that you have about the Teacher of Righteousness, you have a Christ-like teacher in the Teacher of Righteousness. Then in James you have a sort of Christ-like teacher in James the Just. So you have these many Christ types at that time when they were expecting a Messiah and expecting a successful revolt against the Romans.

Miracles in the Dead Sea Scrolls and the Bible

JM: Are there any miracle stories in the Dead Sea Scrolls?

AS: No! No, none. Absolutely not one. I have not read any. The only miracle stories you have are the stories from the Old Testament. Those are old. Those are the stories of the Prophets, the stories of Moses, and so on.

JM: Prophecies expect miracles, do they not?

AS: Yes. They would expect miracles in the future. But there are no miracle stories in the Dead Sea Scrolls. You have what are called the Apocryphal Pseudepigraphic writings. You have miracle stories there about Noah and so on. but as far as miracles in the lives of the Essenes themselves, they were not living miraculous lives. They were not raising the dead.

They were not casting out demons, as any exorcist would do at that time. Such practices would not be considered miraculous during this time. Laying on of hands would be of the same classification of practice and not miraculous. Miracle stories, none, none like you see about Jesus. There is no raising of the dead, there is no multiplication of loaves and fishes. How they got all their food to the Qumran community — probably they transported it from Jericho on the Dead Sea on boats, and probably a lot was delivered from Jerusalem 15 miles away.

But there are no miracles, no signs and wonders, no coming and going of angels, no wrestling with angels, no secret golden plates given to them with revelations on them, none of that. These were exiles out in the desert reading from holy scriptures, writing holy scriptures, revising the holy scriptures, praying every day, waiting for signs, waiting for the coming of the messiah, watching the stars for the signs in the skies — but no miracles.

JM: If you go back to the very beginnings of the whole concept of the belief systems of the Hebrews — no matter which party, all of them — where would you suspect that would come from? We are given, of course, to understand that all of it, whatever particular party of Hebrews you are talking about, Sadducees, Pharisees, Herodians, whatever, each one would claim that theirs was the understanding of God. God's religion and God's direction is exhibited in their beliefs. Where would you suspect that all of these belief systems have come from?

AS: In the recent archeological lectures that I have gone to at the University of Judaism in Bel Air, California, all the rabbis who talk there have fully admitted that the Hebrews were most likely a collection of many groups that lived in the Fertile Crescent, Palestinian area of what we call today Judea and Samaria. They were there long before Moses, whether the historical figure of Moses or the mythological figure of Moses.

Most rabbis and archeologists today do not believe that there ever was an exodus from Egypt. They believe that the indigenous people of Jordan and that area worshipped gods. One god was called "El" over here, another god somewhere else was called "El Adon." Or you have "Adonai." Or you had "Elohim," many "Els," plural. And they were usually a collection of idolatrous cows that they were worshipping in their temple. A lot of these little cows or little bull shrines have been dug up. You can find them in museums throughout the Middle East now.

These people were called probably the "Ha-bi-ru." Some were nomads, some were settled in cities, some lived in the hills and worshipped the god of the hills, some lived in the valleys and worshipped a god who was powerful in the valley. Melchizadek was a priest of one god; I believe his name was "El-Eleyon." Then you have Abraham who was worshipping some other god that he met in Ur, which means "life," Ur of the Chaldees. You have all these people coming together eventually, slowly but surely, forming themselves into tribes, uniting the various tribal gods into one god who was the god of all the tribes.

Every group makes up stories about themselves, so they borrowed from all the mythologies around them, from the Assyrians, from the Babylonians, and the Philistines and the Egyptians, and they put together their flood stories, their god stories, and their Yahweh story.

If you read the Yahweh story as it has been put together by Dr. Harold Bloom, it is called *The Book of J.* You have the most childish god you can imagine — a god that gets hungry, a god that gets mad, a god that will kill you if you do not circumcise your son. He has temper tantrums, he changes his mind. Then you have the Elohim stories which are the stories of the gods and the creation stories, and the stories of the floods. All these were the shared stories that were borrowed by the Hebrews and put into their collective consciousness. Many of these things evolved into what is called the Torah, sometime after the reign of Solomon. These Yahweh stories and Elohim stories were united and put together in the Torah.

Then you have the Writings that were very popular after Solomon, Rehoboam and all that crowd. The Temple priesthood was becoming more powerful, so they put together Leviticus, and added more priestly stories to the Scriptures. Because they owned them, they could write them, revise them, add to them, and drop what they did not like, which is what all biblical scholars admit has happened. There are textual evidences for this.

Later on during one of the reigns of the Kings of Judah, all of a sudden in the Temple, out of the clear blue sky, you suddenly have appearing the book of Deuteronomy. The king comes out in the name of all that is holy, he reads the book of Deuteronomy and adds that to the canon of the Scriptures.

Later on you have the prophets who are trying to battle idolatry and the ways of the pagans, so you have the writings of the Prophets added to the written tradition of the Judeans. So that is where the Hebrews came from. They evolved in that area. It is becoming more and more clear now that as more scientific, archeological, and physical evidences of the bones and stones are put together, the story makes more sense than what we have in the Scriptures.

JM: What is the superiority of the modern-day understanding of Judaism as opposed to any of the other Semitic groups, cults, religions of the Egyptians, Phoenicians, Canaanites, Babylonians — what makes what we call today the Hebrew religion of Judaism far, far superior to anything that has ever existed on the earth?

AS: What makes it superior is that it survived. It is not superior in itself. Any of the other religions that you just listed, if they had survived along with Judaism, or if they had been able to totally supplant Judaism, then we would be talking about their superiority.

What could have happened in the Fertile Crescent area, from Egypt to Mesopotamia, is what happened in India. In India today you have the survival of the pagan religions up to this day. You have the monkey gods. You have the elephant god; and the Krishnas, which are the Christ figures. You have the Ashrams, the monasteries. You have a huge literary tradition thousands of years old in the Upanishads. You have the heretical offshoots called Buddhism. Then you have the tradition of the *Sutras* in writing, the Buddhist scriptures. All of them share some beliefs, revising others.

What happened in India and the Far East could easily have happened in Egypt, Mesopotamia, Babylon and Assyria. We could have all those religions today. There is no reason why we could not have a temple of Isis in downtown Los Angeles. We have temple of Quan Yuen. What is the difference? I could take anyone right now to Hacienda Heights where they have a huge Buddhist temple. And they have the Bodasatva Hall, where you and I could walk in and there are gorgeous statues of Quan Yuen. And they have Buddhist nuns there burning incense before these statues twenty-four hours a day.

What is the difference between that and worshipping Isis in Rome? There is none. It could easily have happened. There is no reason why the Egyptian religion could not have survived intact with their priesthood and their idols and their temple scrolls to this day. None at all. It is just pure chance.

JM: So then there is no real superiority, spiritually speaking?

AS: I see none. There is no moral high ground that the Hebrews had that was not shared by their neighbors. The Egyptians, Babylonians, Greeks, and the Romans all had their morality. They all had laws. They all had courts of justice. They all had standards for righteous behavior. They were not living in chaos. Their cities were orderly. Their tradesmen were as honest as you would find anywhere among the Hebrew people. They had justice, They had capital punishment for people who stole, they had punishments for people who lied. You name it, they had moral standards that were just as high as anything you would find in the Old Testament.

JM: What about this concept that we have been given to understand in this country that the Hebrews were the very, very first people, at their very inception, the worshippers of only one god. Only one deity has ever been the god of the Hebrews, that one divine holy Father. What is the actual history of the Hebrew and that whole nation of Judaism in relation to their gods? How many gods did they in fact really worship?

AS: Even in the Old Testament you have many gods that Israelites worshipped. When the Israelites came out of Egypt, they were worshipping Yahweh for a while. However, when they were getting unhappy they built the Egyptian calf of the goddess Hathor. They immediately reverted to what they were familiar with, and they had a priesthood right there, who was Aaron, who performed the sacrifices and offered the incense to Hathor, the goddess of Egypt.

When the Hebrews split into Judea and Israel, the northern kingdom, Israel, had two temples, one at Dan and the other at Bethel, both containing golden calves that were their gods. They took these gods seriously. In Jerusalem, in Judea they continued the Temple worship in the tradition of Solomon.

During the time of Solomon, the righteous king, the son of David, he was building pagan temples all over Judea. he was building a pagan temple for each of his wives. He had over a thousand wives and concubines. He was even married to one of the daughters of Pharaoh. She had her temple there in the city of Jerusalem. Even Solomon was very ecumenical for his time. Not only did Solomon build those temples, he worshipped in them. That is in Josephus.

True Religion, the Illusion

JM: What I was thinking is that we are given to understand that the way Jehovah's Witnesses and Mormons and the modern-day Masonic cults would explain the different gods that you were talking about, they would say, yes that is true, but you see they got away from the original teachings, from their original God who was the almighty God, the Father, Yahweh. And when they got away from that, then they fell into all this pagan idolatry. So, yes that is true, they were pagans, they did have all those pagan gods, but that was because they fell away from the "true" worship.

What I am talking about is at the very day one, with the true worship. If you go all the way back to day one, there never was any true worship. There were always different gods — Philistine gods, Palestinian gods, Babylonian gods, Samarian gods — the Hebrews were no special people that had only one divine Father. But as you said, that which we call Hebrew is just a collection of all of them?

AS: That is right. Anybody that today, the Jehovah's Witnesses, the Mormons, the Seventh Day Adventists, who have that very narrow view that there always was a pure religion from day one to today, are simply wrong. There is no talking to them, so I do not talk to them. This is one reason why I do not talk to Mormons, because they believe, for example, that the gospel of Jesus Christ was preached to Adam. What? This is ridiculous. If someone is going to sit and look at you with a straight face and say that the gospel of Jesus Christ was preached to Adam, that ends the conversation. There is no talking to someone like that. If they have so little sense of history and sense of what archeology has brought to us in the last hundred years about biblical archeology, then there is no talking to them. It is just time to get up, politely excuse yourself, and go home. It is a waste of time.

JM: That is precisely the point I was making, when you said that those who would stick to the story that there was an original, unblemished, true religion of the almighty God, that all this paganism came in on top of it. What I am saying, is in fact correct. Am I right in assuming there never was a true and correct religion, ever, on the face of the earth? All of what we call Hebrew came out of all the others to start with.

AS: Every modern scholar that I know of today admits that the idea of God has evolved like every other thing and cultural artifact has evolved. There is an excellent book out by Karen Armstrong called *The History of God*, which traces the idea of God from earliest times, from ancient Egypt and other cultures, up through the present, and how God has changed according to the needs of the tribes, or the needs of the nation-state, or the needs of the theologians of the Middle Ages. God has changed and has been revised, and rewritten, and reborn in a way that they have needed.

There is book out, *Christianity* by Hans Küng. He points out in Church history, from the time of Jesus to the present, how the Catholic Church, and later the Protestant Churches, have had paradigm shifts in their teachings: from early Judaism, to Jewish Christianity, to paganized Christianity, to the debates over the nature of Jesus — did he have one nature, two natures, three natures, was he a ghost, was he pure man? Then the Pope decides, yes, he was God and man in a trinity. You finally get all these formulas, these paradigm shifts, and then there are more shifts during the Middle Ages, depending on where science is going, where the church is going, you have more dogmas that never existed three hundred years before, papal infallibility, primacy of one pope over all other bishops.

None of these things were important or even thought of two hundred years before, but all of a sudden, there is a paradigm shift, then everybody must believe that or be killed. These paradigm shifts go on and on. These paradigm shifts are being analyzed, and admitted to, and being dissected in our modern world. I think we are going to see big changes in mainstream Christianity. It is not going to be just Bishop John Shelby Spong writing books denouncing the virgin birth and the resurrection stories as ancient mythological creations, it is going to be so widespread that the churches are going to change radically.

Prophecies of the Dead Sea Scrolls

JM: I think you are correct on that. Did the Dead Sea Scrolls have any prophecies in them?

AS: Yes. They believed in the coming of two messiahs. They believed that they would lead a war against the Kittim which they considered to be the Romans, and they would be backed up by angels and the power of heaven and they would be successful. They knew exactly how long the war would be. They would have a certain number of battles. They would lose two battles, then they would be successful in the others.

They planned on taking over the entire world. There would be no Roman empire, no Egyptian empire, no Greek empire. It would be the rule of God through them, with them being the only survivors in the whole world.

JM: Did they consider themselves the stone of Daniel that would crush the Gentile empires of the world?

AS: I do not remember them using that imagery or expression, but yes, they were going to be the only survivors and all the unright-eous and all the unbelievers were going to die. It would be just like Noah's time. The Essenes out in the desert believed they were like the new ark. They were going to be the survivors and every-one else was going to die. They were going to be the ones repopulating the whole earth with the righteousness of the Lord. There were going to be no pagan temples, no Roman emperors, no taxation, or bad things.

JM: All Gentiles were going to die?

AS: All were going to be dead, except for the righteous few gentiles who were with the Essenes, the conquerors. They would live, but all the other Gentiles would die, all of them.

JM: This sounds exactly like Jehovah's Witnesses philosophy. Everybody in the whole world is going die except the handful that Jehovah has picked and the righteous gentiles.

AS: That is where they got it. It is called the Essene hypothesis. That is what they believed. When it did not happen and the Romans were defiling their scrip-tures and burning the Temple, they got discouraged.

JM: In other words, "I don't see things going our way. They're not supposed to do this, Willis." This whole eschatology, the end-time, last days scenario basi-cally could be traced back to the Essenes also?

AS: Exactly. This view of the future was unique with the Essenes. The Pharisees did not share it. The Sadducees did not share it. The Sadducees, the Herodian Sadducees as opposed to the Sadducees out in Qumran, would have been perfectly content for everything to just go on with them cooperating with the Romans, doing the Temple sacrifices, keeping a lid on the rebellion. People were to pay their taxes, farm the fields, just be good little Jews, and not make any waves.

The Pharisees wanted to do their little thing. They were the internationalists. The Pharisees were the ones who would live in Rome, Greece, and Egypt. They had the synagogues, studied the Torah and the Prophets, and sent their offerings to the Temple in Jerusalem. But they did not really need the Temple; they had their own religion that worked for them. They were doing just fine. They were not looking forward to this huge eschatology. They did not see that in the Scriptures.

It was only the Essenes who were the fanatics, and their allies the Zealots, the *Sicarii*, were part of their group thinking; even if they were not living with them in community, they were part of the thinking. They did the dirty work, the rebellion, and the Essenes joined them when the Zealots really got off the ground.

JM: Then this idea about the "end-times" and "last days" scenario I have always believed that it was based on astrology, on an astrological conclusion of a period of time, like the end of an astrological "age."

AS: Yes. Exactly. That would fit in with the Essene thinking. They believed that they were coming to the end of an age, the end of these things, and the begin-ning of new things. They thought they were going to live. In fact they had that old 40-year baloney thing that has been very popular in thinking. Let me read that one small section to you. This is the Commentary on Psalms.

A little while
and the wicked shall be no more.
I will look towards this place,
but he shall not be there.

JM: Where is that coming from?

AS: Psalms 37:7a–10.

JM: That is directly from the canonical Book of Psalms?

AS: Yes.

JM: Because the Jehovah's Witnesses love to quote that particular verse.

AS: That is the word of the Psalm; now here is the interpretation, what the Essenes say: "Interpreted, this concerns all the wicked at the end of the 40 years. They shall be blotted out and not an evil man shall be found on earth." Is that rather sweeping? Jesus taught, "Many now living shall not die." This is what they believed. This is believed to be first-century interpretation of the Psalms by the Essenes.

JM: Did they have a concept of a "millennium" or a thousand-year period?

AS: They spoke of ages.

JM: Ages, olam in Hebrew.

AS: Yes, ages. They did not say millennium, they said "ages."

JM: Back to the 40 year period. According to Rabbi Berg, one of the Rabbis dealing with the Kabbalah, 40 is a very important number for mystical reasons. It has nothing to do with the calendar at all. It has to do with the mystical. There were 40 days of rain in Noah's flood, Jesus goes into the desert for 40 days, there were 40 years of this, the Israelites were in the wilderness for 40 years. The rabbis I have talked with said this was all a kabbalistic number and that it did not mean 40 literal years, it was that 40 was a mystical metaphor for something. When I am reading that the Essenes said that at the end of 40 years this and that is going to happen, they were still into the mysticism.

AS: Yes. There is a huge amount of mysticism in the Dead Sea Scrolls. Like Episcopal Bishop James Pike, I would call it "misty-cism." They really got themselves in a lot of trouble.

Visions in the Dead Sea Scrolls

JM: Are there visions in the Dead Sea Scrolls?

AS: Yes! All they have is visions. Let me tell you some of the visions. They are not worth anything. They are the usual garbage visions of Old Testament baloney.

JM: They are just filled with it?

AS: Yes, they are full of it. The Words of Moses, Moses Apocryphon, Pseudo-Moses, Samuel Apocryphon, Words of the Heavenly Lights, The Triumph of Righteousness, Vision of the Seductress, Exhortation to Seek Wisdom, Bless My Soul, Songs of the Sage, Lamentations — yes, they had visions galore.

Curses of Satan and his Law, Curses of Melkiresha, which is the Evil One. Visions, lots of visions.

JM: The visions provided the evidence for the Essene interpretation of Scripture?

AS: Evidence, encouragement. They believed that they were being blessed and that they were the only ones in touch with Yahweh and that nobody else was in touch with Yahweh except them.

JM: Did they consider their visions and their writings on an equal level with Scripture? Did they consider their writings to be Scripture?

AS: Yes. They buried all this stuff together. They had a very broad view of authoritative writing. They did not use the word "scripture" or "canon." The highest, of course, would be the Torah. That is major.

They were like the Mormons of their day. You know how Mormons today have the Bible, and *The Book of Mormon*, the *Doctrine and Covenants*, and the *Pearl of Great Price*. The Essenes had the Bible, and this Dead Sea Scrolls body of materials. They kept adding more psalms, more interpretations of Scripture. They kept adding more visions of Joseph, the son of Jacob. These kinds of stories; stories from the Persian court, more cursings of the unbelievers, more exorcisms of the evil one and their works in the world. They continued to add material, hymns, liturgies, and wisdom poetry as it is called in our terminology today. More sacred Scriptures from Yahweh, more letters from heaven.

JM: Are there debates or discussions similar to what is in the Talmud?

AS: They did hair-split in M.M.T. which is the letter they sent to the leaders in Jerusalem. The format was like this:

- What *you* do is this.
- *We* say you should do this; or, this should be done.
- *You* allow offerings from gentiles.
- *We* say it is an offense to accept offerings from gentiles.

They outlined the differences. One difference after another in a rabbinical hair-splitting legalistic way.

JM: The Jehovah's Witnesses claim that all that is in the Dead Sea Scrolls proves that the books of the Bible as we have it today are equally as accurate —

AS: Yes.

JM: — because they are found in the Dead Sea Scrolls.

AS: Yes. Fundamentalists say that also. I have heard that in one Dead Sea Scrolls lecture that I heard at a fundamentalist church. They say the Dead Sea Scrolls prove the Bible and our faith as we have it today. Yes. They say it with total seriousness. So do Mormons.

How somebody who has read the Dead Sea Scrolls, and I am sure that man has, can get up in front of hundreds of people, that was a full audience, and say that. I love it.

JM: According to the Dead Sea Scrolls this whole thing about the Temple being rebuilt in Jerusalem, the Temple of Solomon is going to be rebuilt as a fulfillment of God's holy promise and all that stuff.

AS: A better, bigger, purified temple. It will be beautiful.

JM: Was the Temple of the Temple Scroll distinct from the Temple in the book of Ezekiel?

AS: Ezekiel temple. It is basically the same.

JM: The Temple Scroll was providing details for the Ezekiel temple?

AS: Yes, a large number of details. How wide and how tall the arches would be, that kind of stuff.

JM: The idea of the need to rebuild the Temple. Where did that idea come from?

AS: As far as I know, they really did not expect the Second Temple to be destroyed. But they do talk about rebuilding the Temple. I have the Temple Scroll in front of me.

JM: Once the Essenes took over Jerusalem, they would rebuild the Temple?

AS: Once they took over they would purify it. It was my understanding that they did have an opportunity to do this. I believe, and this is not held by anybody else as far as I know. When the Zealots captured Jerusalem as the first revolt was underway, Jerusalem and the surrounding area were in Zealot hands. Annas and his crowd were killed, and the Zealot appointed High Priest, the new High Priest, was probably one of the Sadducees from the Qumran community. They believed the same thing. They were in the same political and theological camp. So it makes sense that they would choose a righteous zealous priest, a Sadducee, and a son of Zadok to be the new High Priest when the rebellion happened. They reinstituted sacrifices during the rebellion. They had their chance and they failed.

JM: How would the Essenes and the writers of the Dead Sea Scrolls view the State of Israel today?

AS: I believe — this is hindsight and I am not Jewish — I think the *Mia Shaharim*, the ultra-orthodox group is too fanatical on this situation. I think a good Jew, whether he is a zealot or ultra-orthodox like the Essenes, would be happy to see the land of Israel in Jewish hands, even if they are not ultra-orthodox hands. The men who rule Israel right now, while they have an alliance with the ultra-orthodox community as opposed to the Reconstructionists, Conservative and Reform Jews, they are really pretty secular. Those men are secular Jews.

To have the State of Israel, I think that is absolutely fabulous, historically speaking. Now what their attitude would be, they were so independent at the time, the time of Jesus in first-century Judaism. To have an Israel that is not at the mercy of the Roman empire, or the Greek empire, or the Egyptian empire, it would be a dream come true. An independent Israel. That is absolutely unheard of, except during the times of David.

Almost all the other kings who succeeded David had to form alliances with the surrounding empires or get crushed. They really were just vassal states.

JM: Is there any hard, legitimate, *de jure* evidence that either Abraham, Moses, David, or Solomon were actual human beings who actually lived?

AS: There is one piece of archeological evidence that was discovered recently, a stele that mentions the House of David. So that made the fundamentalist, Bible literalists happy. You could consider him mythological. That was a plus.

About the patriarchs Abraham, Isaac and Jacob, there is no evidence for them, they could be mythological figures based on legends.

JM: Two reasons why I ask that. Rabbi Antelman said to me that Abraham, Isaac and Jacob were nothing more than the Father, Son and Holy Ghost, the triune trinity, the triune concept in all ancient religions of the whole world. Rama-Vishnu-Shiva, Horus-Osiris-Isis, the triune principle in all religions of the ancient world. The Hebrews had their triune god Abraham-Isaac-Jacob. The mere fact that there would be any legitimate piece found saying that, what was it? A House of David?

AS: House of David was one line that they found in the stele that was giving the political situation at that time. The House of David was mentioned.

JM: I suspect that does not necessarily have to mean that there was a King David. There is something about the phrase "the House of David" that I question what that means.

AS: Yes. It is open to question.

JM: What did that mean?

AS: There have been books written about the wars of David being borrowed stories from the wars of the Pharaohs. Those books are available at theological libraries. That is an interesting idea, that the stories of David that we have in the Bible are really the stories of Pharaoh with the name of David inserted.

JM: That is what I was thinking. Therefore, anything that would talk about "The House of" David, I have run across too much information over the years talking about "the House of" Rothschild, "the House of" Hanover. In occult circles there is the term "the House of" meaning "the concept of," not necessarily the actu-al house, but it is like "the house of Aquarius," "the house of Pisces." Maybe it was a conceptual idea, a political idea, a sociological idea and it was not in fact a man named David. Maybe "The House of David" implied a particular philosophy or something.

AS: Could be. It is as good a speculation as anything.

JM: What would you say for the whole question of the Dead Sea Scrolls sup-porting Christianity as we know it today? The whole of the Dead Sea Scrolls being offered as the final proof for the validity of Christianity today. Why should Christianity be delighted as punch to have found the Dead Sea Scrolls?

AS: First of all, Christianity. The people who have been in control of the Dead Sea Scrolls and mainstream Christian authorities are not delighted to have the Dead Sea Scrolls. I have heard theologians at the School of Theology at Claremont say that they wish that the Dead Sea Scrolls, when they were found, had been tossed into the Dead Sea. They have caused nothing but problems for an historical study of Christianity.

In fact, Eisenman and his crowd of rebels, Dr. Hugh Schonfield, and Dr. John Allegro, see the Dead Sea Scrolls as being opposition scriptures to the New Testament. They see the Dead Sea Scrolls being the scriptures of what the Essenes call themselves, "the Men of the New Covenant," to be in opposition to the New Covenant of the New Testament. The Dead Sea Scrolls are older than the New Testament. The rituals of the Dead Sea Scrolls, which are similar to early Christianity, are older than Christianity. It has been a big problem. So there is no reason for someone who has read the Dead Sea Scrolls and is a traditional ortho-dox Christian to be happy that they are here because they do blow apart the foun-dations of traditional Christianity. You will hear that you can read into the Dead Sea Scrolls pretty much anything you want to.

JM: Just like the Bible.

AS: We could have this room here filled with ten people, all with Ph.Ds. in early Church history. One has his Ph.D. from a Baptist Seminary. One from Brigham Young University. One from Loma Linda University. One from the Gregorian University in Rome. One from Concordia University. You will have ten different authoritative and well-educated views on the origin of Christianity. They will all have their own proofs on why they are right and textual evidences for why they are right. You will have different, and radically different, opposing viewpoints.

THE TRUTH AND MYSTERY OF GNOSIS
By Paul Tice

Truth is always individual, anyone else's truth is worthless. Truth is a non-transferable ticket which only bears one name.

—Yatri

The passion for truth is silenced by answers which have the weight of undisputed authority.

—Paul Tillich

O seekers, remember all distances are traversed by those who yearn to be near the source of their being.

—Kabir

The truth and the mystery concerns who we really are. We know there is an ultimate truth to humanity, regarding who we really are — we just don't collectively understand it yet. That is the mystery. Gnosis, or the illumination of knowledge on a deep, personal level, can begin to reveal the answers. Gnosticism is a faith now nearly forgotten but it has become clear in the previous chapters that it was rather common in the first four centuries of Christianity. It was considered a heresy by those who opposed it — those mainly being the fathers of the Church. But it did have value.

Gnosis in Greek means knowledge, or to know. This does not refer to factual knowledge, but to an intuitive or spiritual understanding that comes from experience. The early Gnostics were mystics, people who knew that you could experience God for yourself instead of going into a church and being told what to believe.

In Hebrew, to know means to experience — so, according to the Hebrews, knowing God means to experience Him. This is what most all early Hebrews and Christians were striving to do. Unfortunately, the Church got in the way of personal experience, by creating "organized religion." There's a saying which states, "Religion is for the masses, and mysticism is for the individual." If you want to be a sheep and follow along with the masses to get a generic, candy-coated version of your spirituality, then follow the teachings of the Christian fathers. If you want to explore your own individual spirituality, you must go deeply inside yourself, instead of through church doors.

"Wait a minute," you might say. "Why can't I do both?" You most certainly can. But prioritize the matter. You are a unique person with your own unique spiritual path — here on this Earth for a reason. No one else is here for that same purpose. You are special. Find your reason for being here and don't let others decide it for you.

No man ever followed his genius till it misled him.
—Henry David Thoreau

These soul-searching ideas threatened the Church. If you want organized religion, you can't have people "doing their own thing." The Gnostics did not bow down to any Earthly authority or dogma because each person must find that authority *within*, as he or she strives to attain gnosis. With this idea growing during the first two centuries of Christianity, something had to be done. The organized church persecuted and stamped out the Gnostic movement so that by the fourth century all Gnostic churches had been closed and all known writings destroyed. Yet the Gnostics are recognized today as having been brilliant depth psychologists and, in a broader sense, possibly the first religious philosophers. Their importance was never recognized until centuries later. Edward Gibbon, in his legendary book called the *Decline and Fall of the Roman Empire* said, "The Gnostics were distinguished as the most polite, the most learned, and the most wealthy of the Christian name." In exchange for their greatness, they were ruthlessly persecuted by the Church.

Reign of Confusion

The Church was in terrible disarray for centuries, and is not the great authority it makes itself out to be. It stumbled its way to its current position of authority, then used violence to insure its standing. It took the Church 150 years after the death of Jesus to establish the present system of deacons, priests, and bishops. One hundred years later the clergy was still determining which form of Christianity should be the accepted form, but there were still great differences of opinion.

By the year C.E. 325, the Roman Emperor Constantine decided to convene the Council of Nicea to settle the problem once and for all for the entire Roman Empire. All bishops were present except for the Bishop of Rome, due to his advanced age (however, he sent two representatives). This Council was one of the most manipulative meetings in the history of the world (see *History of the First Council of Nice*, by Dean Dudley, reprinted by The Book Tree). The bishops were told how they were expected to vote beforehand, and all those who disagreed were excommunicated, removed from the meeting by armed guards, and banished to remote islands. The Council continued its business, Constantine's theology was presented to the remaining bishops, and it received unanimous approval. What a surprise. What resulted was Christianity, in large part, as we know it today.

After all this was over, an official version of the New Testament *still* did not exist. This did not matter to Constantine. They had decided on a general theology, so a police authority was immediately sent out to burn and destroy all religious material which did not agree with the new, official theology. Athanasius, a contemporary to all this, was born around C.E. 296 and died in 373. (He followed Constantine's example in 367, ordering the expulsion of heretics and all their books from monasteries — thereby causing the greatest known collection of Gnostic writings, the Nag Hammadi Library, to be buried. This had immediately followed the Synod of Laodicea, in around 363 in Phrygia, which chose the initial books of the canon for the first time in history.) He was apparently present at the Council of Nicea, but because of his relative youth and lack of status, was not allowed to speak. Yet it was his views on Christ's deity which eventually became the official doctrine of the Church sometime after his death. Before this, during his 45 year reign as Bishop of Alexandria, he was exiled five different times by five different emperors because of his views, for a grand total of 17 years. After the second time, he probably kept his bags packed.

Later, in the year 389 by edict of the Emperor Theodosius, the library of Alexandria, Egypt, was burned to the ground. This was the greatest loss of valuable information in the history of the world. It was the world's greatest library, containing over 700,000 manuscripts, scrolls, and codices — most of them without duplicates. The entire purpose of the library had been envisioned by Alexander the Great — to house all of the books ever written under one roof. Some of these ancient documents, 270,000 of them, had been collected by Ptolemy Philadelphus in exchange for rich rewards. Can you imagine what knowledge and value these works had? These works were allegedly burned because many of them contained the doctrinal basis of the Gospels. In other words, the truth. Can you imagine what 700,000 ancient documents, gathered in one place, would look like?

About the year 393 (and with many great Gnostic works now destroyed) the clergy made a more accurate decision on what books to use for the New Testament following the Synod at Hippo in Africa. This canon was meant to represent the official religion that had been crammed down their throats 75 years earlier by Constantine. To this day, the books we find in the New Testament have never been declared official by any authority or council. The disagreement over New Testament books continued for centuries. The Book of Revelation, today considered the most important New Testament book, had continually been taken in and out of the Bible for over a thousand years.

Once the Gnostics were finally defeated with the fall of the Manichaeans around C.E. 600, the Dark Ages soon followed. This bleak period began largely because Christian leaders acted on a realization — that to control the people and avoid additional centuries of trouble, it was necessary to control knowledge and its dissemination. All the ancient wisdom that could be gathered together and either destroyed or hidden away in places like the Vatican Library, would be taken out of circulation. All avenues which people might take to achieve independent learning were closed off. Not even priests or prelates were allowed to learn to read or write during many Dark Age years. Even bishops were just barely able to spell (in Latin), while all sources of true knowledge, which could potentially threaten the Church, were kept away from them. Much of the great knowledge of the past is allegedly locked away in the enormous Vatican Library, where no one to this day, except the private "guardians," have access to it.

The practice of controlling knowledge was refined by Pope Paul IV in 1555 soon after he graduated from being inspector-general of the Inquisition and became pope. At this time he established the Index of Forbidden Books, in which every book considered to be detrimental would be blacklisted and in some cases stored away and forbidden to be seen by any Christian (or anyone else for that matter). The pope warned that anyone who read a book on the list was committing a mortal sin. After more than four centuries the Index was "discontinued" by Pope Paul VI in 1966. It would seem that many rare and interesting books may still be in the Vatican's possession. If anyone has a Vatican Library card, I'd like to borrow it for a few months.

The Papacy — A Sham?

What kind of authority does the papacy really have? The entire development of the papacy comes from very dubious origins and early popes were scorned by respected Church authorities like Tertullian. Jesus himself was against calling any man "father," which is what the word "pope" really means. Pope Cyprian, in the mid 250's scoffed at the idea that his own position "holds the succession from Peter."

The name "pope" only started to be used at the beginning of the third century, and from the third to fifth centuries applied to *all* bishops. It was when Cyprian was being called the "bishop of bishops," and "the blessed Pope," that he took offense. Finally, in the sixth century, the term pope became reserved for the bishops of Rome. In the year 1073 a Roman Council officially banned anyone else from using the title. So was Peter the first "pope?" No. He was just another bishop (if that) and I agree with Cyprian — that the succession from Peter is a sham. Some will argue this point and look to the Bible for proof.

> He saith unto them, "But whom say ye that I am?"
> And Simon Peter answered and said, "Thou art the Christ,
>   the Son of the living God."
> And Jesus answered and said to him, "Blessed art thou,
>   Simon Bar-Jona: for flesh and blood has not revealed it to thee,
>   but my Father which is in heaven."
> And I say also to thee, "That thou art Peter, and upon this rock I will
>   build my church: and the gates of hell shall not prevail against it."
> *Matthew 16:15–18*

When this argument comes up, people quote Matthew 16:18 and leave out the three previous verses. We should remember that after meeting Jesus, Simon Bar-Jona had changed his name to Peter (or Cephas, meaning "rock,") due to his strong faith.

But the main point is that Jesus was not referring to Peter when he spoke of building his "church." Jesus spoke Aramaic. In Aramaic "upon this rock" can also mean "upon this truth." The *Geneva Bible* translates "rock" as "true faith, which confesses Christ." Although the words for "Peter" and "rock" are the same in the original language, Jesus reminds Peter what his name is *first*, then says that upon this truth he will build his Church. He is complimenting Peter for having confessed this truth in verse 16. The Church will not be built upon Peter, it will be built upon "truth." It is now agreed by not only many Protestants, but by many Roman Catholics that this is the more likely interpretation (for example, see *The Bishop of Rome*, by Jean Tillard).

Jesus often used a play on words in his teachings. This was a pun, of sorts, and a compliment as well. The two words were the same, but used differently by Jesus in a rather nice gesture toward Peter.

When these two words/verses were translated into the Greek, they were also translated as two distinct and separate words, bringing into question Peter's authority. Jesus himself rebuked Peter only five verses later. This resulted after Peter had reproached Jesus for predicting to his disciples his own suffering and death. Peter insisted that it would not happen. Jesus told him:

> Get thee behind me, Satan: thou art an offence unto me; for thou savourest not the things that be of God, but those that be of men.
>
> *Matthew 16:23*

It's unlikely that Jesus would have entrusted the future of his church to a man he had just addressed in this way.

Returning to verse 18, we should also be aware that in the Aramaic language there was no word for "church" at that time. Jesus repeatedly told his followers that they must not have temples, priests, synagogues, or services. The Greek word, *ecclesie* or *ekklesia*, was used since it was the closest to the Aramaic, and meant, at that time, a "public meeting." So Jesus was okay with having public meetings, but did not desire to have temples, priests, or services. He clearly knew that he was building a following, but had no intention of founding a "church," as we know it today.

In order to legitimize the papacy we must prove that Peter not only lived in Rome, but was a bishop there. This is the Catholic claim. Most authorities today state there is no reason to believe that Peter was ever in Rome, much less being a bishop there. More than 20 different references from respected scholars affirm this. For instance, Charles Du Moulin was an ecclesiastical lawyer from the mid 1500's who was considered a faithful and steadfast Roman Catholic. He said, "Even when, after the breaking up of the empire, the Bishops of Rome began to extend their authority over other Churches, they never alleged or put forth this story of Peter's being in Rome; the story, I suppose, not having yet been invented."

From *The Popular and Critical Bible Encyclopedia*, vol. 3, from 1908, we find,

> **1. Peter in Rome.** The most thorough investigation of noted scholars has shown — that there is not even a remote tradition (after Peter's death) for the first century — to prove that Peter was ever in Rome. In fact there are no such assertions until after the beginning of the third century, in any document of authentic note.

Yet our modern Catholic literature continues to defend it.

This topic was covered to show that true spiritual authority resides within you, rather than in tradition. Man-made authority is artificial and counterfeit. Your authority is found within the power of your own spirit.

Church Improvisations

None of the Gospels of Matthew, Mark, Luke, or John were written by these people. Authorship of these books were *assigned* to them because they had known

Jesus. In other words, the disciples (followers) were made into apostles (teachers) by the Church, by assigning their names to the Gospels. This was a major step for the Church in becoming organized. Without the apostles, the Church would have no way to connect its history to Jesus in any legitimate way. This was so important that the Church, for example, "legitimized" the authorship of Mark with the testimony that Eusebius said that Papias said that John (the Presbyter) said that Mark wrote down what Peter said that Jesus said. Once Gospel authors were assigned, the Church had some "legitimacy."

During the time of Constantine in around C.E. 313, Christianity was still struggling to come into its own. By 4th Century standards, a religion was not considered legitimate unless it had an appropriate "charter." Therefore, the Old Testament was officially coupled with the New Testament to serve this purpose. This coupling provided Christianity with a more solid historical basis for the various myths and rituals it had incorporated into its system. Antiquity for the religion could be claimed, so additional rationalizations were incorporated, connecting these two belief structures more solidly (something Irenaeus had begun over a century earlier). This coupling provided Christianity with the legitimacy it so desperately needed. I believe this is something that Jesus would have opposed, based on his view of God the Father.

During the first four centuries, the Church had argued bitterly over how the Gospels should be interpreted. This is something which also would have saddened Jesus. Many doctrinal questions were settled and are still accepted today without any basis on the teachings of Jesus. Throughout the centuries, Christianity has spent far more time engaged in violence for the purpose of promoting ideas that were completely made up, than with following the true teachings of Christ, which were based on nonviolence. This is where we went wrong.

Jesus taught us how to achieve a triumph of the spirit, but we have been led astray by an organization which had other agendas than this. One Church error which is most disturbing is the idea of Jesus being God Incarnate. In *no place* in the Bible does Jesus ever explicitly claim to be the Second Person of the Trinity. Doing so would have made him three entities in one, God Incarnate, but he never claimed this. He never did, nor did his disciples, because the concept of God Incarnate had not yet been invented! Jesus was here on behalf of the Father, and was consistently referred to in the Bible as God's servant.

He called himself the "Son of Man" except in John, where he called himself the "Son of God" (for example, in 9:35-37). He soon explains that having the title does not make him God (John 10:31-38), but subservient — one whom the Father had sanctified and sent into the world. Claiming equality to the heavenly Father would have been blasphemous to Jesus, which explains why he never did it. St. Paul had the highest regard for Jesus, but he never called him God, either. *Jesus never claimed to be God.* Judging from its context, the statement "I and my Father are one," portrays a common goal or purpose to God, and nothing more.

The Trinity itself is an erroneous concept. One cannot find the doctrine of the Trinity spelled out anywhere in the Bible. This was pointed out as early as the eighth century by the theologian St. John of Damascus. The only place we find any reference to the Trinity is in Matthew 28:19–20, when Jesus tells his disciples:

> Go ye therefore, and teach all nations, baptizing them in the name of
> the Father, and of the Son, and of the Holy Ghost.

Scholarship proves with little doubt that this verse was added later. Virtually every modern scholar agrees that the early Church did not baptize anyone using these words, and that the creation of the Trinity and to baptize in its name came much later. The early Church always baptized people in Jesus' name only, and this Bible verse in Matthew, or at least its end part, was clearly inserted at a later time.

The Trinity entered Christian thought through Tertullian. In the C.E. 190s he was studying the Montanist heresy, but had not yet defected and joined them. At this time, Christianity recognized the Father and the Son. The Holy Spirit was also recognized, but rarely mentioned — and never mentioned at all as part of a Trinity. The Montanists were focused solely on the Holy Spirit, even claiming that it was speaking to them through their trance-channel mediums. They were also playing with the idea that God had three separate names or divisions. While Tertullian was known to be studying Montanism, he began emphasizing that the Holy Spirit was divine and began including it with the Father and Son in descriptions of the Trinity. Modern Christians would be shocked to know that today's New Age "channelers" which they try so hard to avoid because they channel under the influence of "demons" or "evil spirits" are, according to early Christian belief, simply under the influence of the Holy Spirit.

Another shadowy Christian belief concerns sin. Where did Jesus say anything to the effect that God would forgive our sins only because of his death on the cross? I am unaware of any such statement. On the contrary, Jesus constantly preached that we could be forgiven by God if we call upon Him with faith and repentance. For example, when he taught his disciples how to pray in Luke 11:1–4, he instruct- ed them to ask God for forgiveness (note also the parables in Luke 15). This, of course, was before any of us were "saved" with his blood. So Jesus was telling us that it was possible to be forgiven by God without him ever having "died for us" yet! This forgiveness would be consistent with an all loving God. My contention is that Jesus came to save us from ignorance, not sin. Apparently, this belief regard- ing sin was adopted from the ancient world, whereby the gods, or God (depending on your religion), needed to be appeased with the blood of a sacrificial victim. Only then would we be "forgiven." This idea was probably incorporated to appease Jews who were not accepting Christ in the early days of Christianity, when the religion was confined to a predominantly Jewish area. This sacrificial necessity is more con- sistent with the Yahweh of Judeo-Christianity than with the Father Jesus spoke of. Our acceptance of this belief is precisely the ignorance which Jesus was fighting to save us from.

Although Christ said God will forgive us without him having yet been sacri- ficed, he is also made to say, in John 16, that his death will actually save us from sin. Why this disparity? The way Jesus taught in the Gospels of Matthew, Mark, and Luke are completely different from what we find in certain sections of John. Rather than parables, we find lengthy discourses recorded in John. Chapters 14–16 are especially suspect by *many* scholars who believe they were added to support the Son of God and virgin birth ideas — both of which were never claimed by Jesus in the Synoptic Gospels.

The virgin birth is clearly a questionable area. Jesus was a special man who surely possessed great wisdom and was inspired by God. If he happened to be born in the normal sense, he deserves just as much respect and admiration by Christians. Many Gnostics believe that something incredible may have happened at or around his baptism rather than at his birth to endow him with such wisdom. Concerning his birth, the genealogies of Christ found in both Matthew and Luke agree that he was the son of David (rather than the Son of God). In the Gospel of Mark it is plainly announced that Jesus had become the Son of God *only at the baptism*, and in Mark's first chapter there is no hint of Jesus ever being the Son of God *before* the baptism. We also find in Romans 1:3–4 that Jesus was born from "the seed of David," and declared to be the Son of God only after his resurrection. So if God "adopted" Jesus at his baptism, or if Jesus was declared God's son following the resurrection, where did this "born of a virgin" tale come from? This story was ram- pant in the ancient world with other faiths. There were many pagan gods before the time of Jesus who were all said to have been born of a virgin. Therefore, it did not take a genius to figure out that pagans would gravitate toward the Christian faith during its formative years if some of the same pagan stories, like the virgin birth, were adopted into it.

If Mary had been a virgin and remained one after Jesus' birth, she would have clearly known that he was someone of great importance. Yet she seems to display no knowledge of the kind. Early in Jesus' ministry, Mary and other relatives show up to apprehend Jesus and take him home because they think he is crazy, or "beside himself." (Mark 3:21) Would Mary have done this if she had given him a virgin birth?

St. Paul never mentions the virgin birth and he reported and wrote on Jesus more than anyone. Peter, who was closest to Jesus, never seemed to know about it either. The Bible, in its *original language*, never predicted the virgin birth or even said that it happened. Although Irenaeus mentioned it in C.E. 190, it was not officially adopted, Church-wide, until C.E. 451 when it was accepted as part of the Nicene Creed!

Modern science proves that if a virgin birth *were* to occur, the offspring would be *female*, not male, because there would be no Y chromosome from the male sperm.

We need to get back to the original teachings of Jesus and the true Church. It is not fair to the spirit of truth, and Jesus himself, to add in all kinds of lies and mythologies. But it was done. Lies have stifled the growth of the spirit, but have allowed the growth of the Church. Lies have manipulated people's beliefs and disallowed spiritual exploration — which is what Jesus was promoting from the start. Jesus was fighting to provide people with a triumph of the human spirit. We will achieve that more easily if we can get back to his original teachings and understand them, especially within the context of the early Church and its political and social agendas.

Christianity is not a bad religion. It's the way its been interpreted and manipulated that's bad. Early Christianity became embroiled in politics and power struggles, and lost the triumph of the spirit which Christ had brought. It became a religion *about* Jesus instead of a religion *of* Jesus. Early in the Christian movement, during the terrible persecutions against them, they heroically stuck together and treated each other as true Christians and brothers.

> They walk in all humility and kindness, and falsehood is not found among them, and they love one another. They despise not the widow, and grieve not the orphan. He that hath, distributeth liberally to him that hath not. If they see a stranger, they bring him under their roof, and rejoice over him, as it were their own brother; for they call themselves brethren, not after the flesh, but after the Spirit and in God; but when one of their poor passes away from the world, and any one of them see him, then he provides for his burial according to his ability; and if they hear that any of their number is imprisoned or oppressed for the name of their Messiah, all of them provide for his needs, and if it is possible that he may be delivered, they deliver him. And if there is among them a man that is poor and needy, and they have not an abundance of necessaries, they fast two or three days that they may supply the needy with their necessary food.
>
> —Aristides (AD 125) on the early Christians

Once the persecutions were over and Christianity had fully developed, we have the following:

> Wild beasts are not such enemies to mankind as are most Christians in their deadly hatred of one another.
>
> —Ammianus Marcellinus, 4th-century historian

By this time, controversy had erupted within the Church over how to interpret

Christ's message, councils were convened to help solve the infighting, and power brokers ultimately instituted all kinds of lies and falsehoods now accepted today. Jesus was not a Christian because he never claimed to be God, never supported the idea of a priesthood, or never claimed to be part of a Trinity, among other things. After the Church created and added things to the story of Christ, it declared itself infallible. Infallible, yet based on falsehoods. In a classic work called *Church History of the Fourth Century*, the author, Mosheim, summed up Christianity's development during the fourth century by stating that "to deceive and lie, when religion can be promoted by it, was a virtue." In other words, lying and embellishing was *encouraged*. It was common practice for religions of the fourth century to employ false information. Only with great courage today could we ever repair the damage. Neander, one of the greatest and most respected Church historians has also said, "Pious frauds overflowed the Church like a flood from the first to the thirteenth century." Today, we are left with the backwash — not only from Christianity but other religions as well. In order to spiritually progress, we need to face these facts. We must remove the denials and claims that "my religion," no matter what it might be, is the true word of God. The true word of God will come through an inner experience, a personal revelation, rather than from the outer shell of a church and/or religious structure. Religions can give guidance, but spirituality gives answers. The focus must shift to a spiritual one, and away from an exclusive, dogmatic one. Dictating what people must believe, and threatening to burn them alive merely for holding an opinion has been a major stumbling block to a triumph of the spirit.

Pulling the Plug on Knowledge

Eusebius lived from C.E. 263–339 and wrote the only surviving historical account of the formation of the Church from someone contemporary to the time (*The History of the Church*). Because of this, he has been used as a primary source by many researchers. The problem with this is that he wrote not from a strictly historical perspective, but from a Christian, and biased, one. He wrote, "I have repeated whatever may rebound to the glory, and suppressed all that could tend to the disgrace of our religion." From the very beginning the Church had suppressed opposing information which, in some cases, could have been more accurate. Based on centuries of repression, it is not surprising that the accounts of Eusebius have survived while others have not.

The Roman Catholic Church, in its confusion and lust for power, has done more to retard human knowledge on this earth than any other institution. This is not a statement aimed at attacking the Church — it is the simple truth. Ernest Renan was conservative in saying, "The triumph of Christianity was the destruction of civil life for a thousand years." General scholarship estimates that book burnings and repression of knowledge by the Church has set us back approximately 2000 years, intellectually. For example, in the sixth century B.C.E. Pythagoras put forth the idea that the earth rotated around the sun. Around 270 B.C.E. a Greek astronomer named Aristarchus went further and *proved* the sun was a gigantic body and that the Earth revolved around it. He did so with an ingenious method of timing the half-moons. This was accepted knowledge for a few centuries, until the Church came along. Without the turmoil of the Dark Ages and its resulting repression, this idea could have grown and flourished. Instead, we lost this knowledge almost completely and it did not resurface until the 16th century (about 2000 years later) through Copernicus, who was persecuted by the Church for reintroducing it.

In the 3rd century B.C.E. the accurate circumference of the Earth had been determined and measured by Eratosthenes, who was the librarian at Alexandria. But the library was burned in 389 C.E. and in the eighth century a bishop named Virgilius tried to reintroduce and promote the idea that the earth was round. He was forced to recant. When Christopher Columbus sailed to America, he was without this scientific knowledge. He did not know for certain that the earth was round, and many sailors of the day feared it was flat and that they might fall off the ends of the earth. Discoveries of new lands were immensely delayed since getting an accurate bearing was a problem. We were missing this knowledge for about 1800 years.

Hipparchus had invented longitude and latitude by the 2nd century B.C.E., but it was never fully used by seafarers until the 1700's. In 1714 the Parliament of England offered a huge reward for solving the problem of determining longitude and it took 50 years, until 1764, before someone succeeded. All told, it took about 1900 years before we came back to the answer. Many such answers were suppressed and lost in the Dark Ages, or had been previously burned by Church authorities. From the fourth century, when Christianity took real power, to the sixth century, Christianity held Grecian philosophy in vassalage — in other words, they allowed it to survive in exchange for its subservience. In the sixth century an Imperial Mandate finally came down and the last schools of Greek philosophy were *shut down.* In Greek, the word philosophy means "the love of Sophia" or "the love of wisdom." It's been estimated (by George Fox, in *The Vanishing Gods*) that if it wasn't for Christianity combined with a few other Dark Ages problems like plagues and barbaric invasions, we could have gone from Eratosthenes to Einstein in eight or nine centuries instead of twenty-three.

> He that takes away reason to make way for revelation puts out the light of both, and does much the same as if he should persuade a man to put out his eyes the better to receive the remote light of an invisible star by a telescope.
>
> —John Locke

Throughout history, the Church has put up a bitter and persistent opposition to astronomy, geology, biology, paleontology, and evolution. At various times she has also banned or prevented the investigation or practice of medicine, surgery, anesthetics, life insurance, agriculture, the census, printing, gravitation, a round Earth, the heliocentric system, geography in general, and the use of steam and electricity. We know that in 1633 Galileo was forced to recant under the threat of death after he discovered and could scientifically *prove* that the earth revolved around the sun. This proof was suppressed for years because the Church believed that the earth was the center of the universe and refused to admit otherwise.

> When, from lack of information, the minds of men cannot freely function, then may a dictator assume control and make himself a god.
>
> —Henry Binkley Stein

In this case, a representative of God. It is good to have spiritual leadership, but that leadership should not be forced upon people under threats of death and torture, and should be based on truth.

Another example of actual truth being overridden by theological "truth" comes from the late nineteenth century. Church authority Father Hardonin urged us to accept his explanation of the earth's rotation (why it spins) in place of science. He said, "The rotation of the earth is caused by lost souls trying to escape from the fire in the center of the earth — which is the wall of hell — thus making the whole revolve, as the squirrel, by climbing, turns its cage."

The Path to God

Remnants of this attitude still exist, but the Church has become more open today. Many people continue to accept its authority blindly without questioning its history. The background of the Church is important. If a man with a criminal past requested to move into your house, would you investigate his past closely, or would you allow him to move in because he told you not to bother to investigate? This attitude began in the Church in the late second century. Church father Tertullian declared that it was no longer necessary to think or reason because God had spoken to us in the Bible, making it completely unnecessary to investigate. He admitted that people who relied on reason and personal experience would reject the doctrines of orthodox Christianity "because they are absurd." Therefore, such doctrines must be accepted on sheer faith. He created a catalogue of vices, calling one of them "the thirst for knowledge," banishing it from the lives of Christians and replacing it with blind faith. To this day, faith takes precedence over knowledge. One of the main goals of religion — any religion — is to get people to accept "the truth" without questioning it. The goal of the spiritual quest, however, is to discover the truth by questioning and exploring.

Some people need to follow a strong authority and be told what to believe. They are not ready for the difficult job of discovering the spiritual knowledge within themselves (where it really resides). For those who are ready, however, the reward is great. When the modern Gnostic, Carl Jung, was asked if he believed in God he answered, "I could not say I believe. I know!" You are either in touch with yourself on a spiritual level, or you grope around, looking "out there" for the answers. God is found within, and this is something the Gnostics knew.

Elaine Pagels in *The Gnostic Paul,* professed that St. Paul operated from many Gnostic principles. In his epistles Paul said that he used two levels of interpretation regarding his teachings, depending on the spiritual level of his listeners. The Platonic Gnostics accepted St. Paul from the beginning because they saw both levels clearly. It is well known by scholars that Paul's genuine epistles were revised by the Church in order to conceal many of his Gnostic views and exclude his celibacy (unlike today, celibacy was frowned upon by the Church in the second century — even for saints like Paul).

Moses Maimonedes, the great Jewish philosopher and Gnostic of the 12th century wrote:

> Every time that you find in our books a tale the reality of which seems impossible, a story which is repugnant to both reason and common sense, then be sure that the tale contains a profound allegory veiling a deeply mysterious truth; and the greater the absurdity of the letter, the deeper the wisdom of the spirit.

To the Gnostic, the spiritual meaning is always more important than whether the tale was true or not. This is one of the reasons why some Gnostic teachings were attacked and destroyed by Christianity — the premise was used that such things could never have happened and were therefore "absurd." Tertullian, as mentioned above, had said the same thing about Christian doctrines, but demanded they be accepted on faith rather than inner exploration or experience.

What else did the Gnostics teach? Balance was important — something that was a necessity to the entire universe. They were not strictly patriarchal as a result, and taught the importance of God the Mother as well as the Father. Men and women shared equally in services and in worship. It seemed only natural to them.

They encouraged creativity and imagination. Things did not necessarily have to be done "by the book." They used other scriptures in addition to the official ones. These other scriptures contained many positive and spiritual truths. Lessons were learned from these other teachings, promoting spiritual growth. Whether the events were true or not didn't matter. They were not interested in teaching history, they were interested in teaching people how to grow spiritually.

To the Gnostics, understanding the inner world as opposed to the outer world resulted in spiritual understanding and a closer relationship to God.

> He who knows himself knows God.
>
> —*Clement of Alexandria*

When we came into this world we retained a small part of divinity. We are part of God — that is why we are capable of finding God within. What we've retained is referred to as the divine spark. It emanates from the energy that empowers the universe and all it contains. The divine spark exists naturally within us, but it has been covered over by this material world, and overcome by the powers within it. The inner search of the Gnostic is to rediscover that lost spark; to care for it and redeem it. It is a personal journey, completely set apart from any creed or dogma. But it can be done.

The Ultimate Con

Instead of seeing a spiritual conflict between God and the Devil, Gnostics believed in a struggle between a true and unknowable God and a lesser god of creation. The Gnostics made a big distinction between the true God and the creator god of this world. The true God is a spiritual force apart from this world. The Creator God broke away from the spiritual realm to create matter and the physical universe. The universe still contains the divine spark in all its elements, but it is masked over and hidden. The Creator God has intentionally covered over this divine spark and the world itself is in darkness.

Do the Gnostics recognize a devil? Only in the persona of the Creator God. His kingdom is one of ignorance, evil, and darkness. We in fact live in this kingdom. It is matter itself that is evil, being the complete opposite of spirit. This is a hard pill to swallow for those adherents of traditional religions, but it makes sense to many such people when they hear it for the first time.

The True God — Power in Spirit

This God beyond God, as theologian Paul Tillich refers to Him, is referred to as the "En Sof" (the limitless or boundless) by the Jewish Kabbalists, and is also found in Taoism. Christ also mentions the true God in "The Secret Book of John":

> Concerning him, the Spirit, it is not fitting to think of him as a God, or that he is of a (particular) sort. For he is more excellent than the gods; he is a dominion over which none rules; for there is none before him, nor does he need them (the gods); he does not even need life, for he is eternal... He is light. He is illimitable, since there is none before him to limit him. [He is] not subject to judgment, since there is none before him to judge. He is not corporeal, he is not incorporeal. He is not great, he is not small. He is nothing at all that exists, but something more excellent than that.

The true God, to the Gnostics, dwells beyond all physical reality and matter. He can influence us only through the divine spark, but that is difficult in this heavy, burdensome world of matter. The true God is only powerful in the realm of spirit — but His presence is clear during great acts of heroism, personal sacrifice, and true kindness. Giving unselfishly and treating others as you yourself would like to be treated are also acts inspired by the true God. This is because no material gains are involved. Nothing of this world is expected as a reward. The reward is in doing something special and meaningful for others (or for yourself). Nothing else is involved.

What movies usually win the Academy Award for best picture? Most commonly they are ones which portray a "triumph of the human spirit." They reflect how people can overcome anything should they simply believe and follow their hearts. "Forrest Gump" and "Gandhi" are two good examples. Even the main characters in the tragic movie "Titanic" experience a great triumph of the spirit. When it happens in real life, instead of in movies, it is an unforgettable experience.

Trapped and Deceived

Most people in this world, however, are focused on material things — goods, products, people, and money. Power and greed spring from the desire to possess or control these goods, products, people, or money. This dog-eat-dog world is not a very nice place. Even in nature we find it. We live on a planet where all its creatures rely exclusively on killing and consuming other living creatures. Some of the ways these other creatures are killed and consumed are extremely vicious and cruel. Would an all-loving God create a place like this? Not likely.

Yahweh, or Jehovah, was the Creator God of this world, according to the Bible. He withheld knowledge from men, starting with the Garden of Eden, where he told Adam and Eve not to eat of the Tree of Knowledge. He lied to them and told them in Genesis 3:3 that "In the day thou eatest thereof thou shalt surely die," referring to the fruit from the tree.

The serpent, in Genesis said:

> Ye shall not surely die. For God doth know that in the day ye eat there-of, then your eyes shall be opened, and ye shall be as gods, knowing good and evil.

Gen. 3:4–5

Considering that Adam lived to be 930 years old, who was telling the truth? Instead of dying when he ate the fruit, Adam's eyes became opened and he became "like a god." Wisdom was bestowed upon Adam and Eve. It came from the serpent. Jesus told his followers, "Be ye wise as serpents," encouraging them to pursue wisdom. Even Saint Augustine considered the serpent wise and Yahweh foolish when he said, "We are ensnared by the wisdom of the serpent; we are set free by the fool-ishness of God."

This was a very good quote, but Augustine had it wrong. He should have said, "We are ensnared by the foolishness of God; we are set free by the wisdom of the serpent."

With Adam and Eve now knowing good and evil, with their eyes opened, Yahweh's evil was exposed. Yahweh had brought evil into the world — and Adam and Eve were now capable of seeing this fact clearly. The concept of a devil did not exist at this time. For the early Hebrews all evil came from God. Yahweh himself admits it:

> I form light and create darkness. I make peace, and *I create evil.*
> I, the Lord, do all these things. (emphasis mine)

Isaiah 45:7

Yahweh, sometimes known as Yaldabaoth, not only endorsed evil, he wa s known as a blind god, totally unaware of any higher power. The following comes from James M. Robinson, editor of *The Nag Hammadi Library*:

> ...Yaldabaoth is not the highest God; his mother Sophia made a cata-strophic miscalculation in conceiving him without her mate — an abortive effort on her part to imitate the first creative act of the high-est God, a presumption punished by the blinding of her son. This blinded, ignorant god is so jealous of the humans he has fabricated that he forbids them to eat from the trees of the garden the food that leads to knowledge and immortality. He is so stupid he cannot even find Adam in the garden, and has to call out and ask, "Where are you?"

So much for an all-knowing god. The Gnostics wanted nothing to do with the worship of this so-called god. An all-loving God does not deceive mankind, attempt to deny them wisdom, bring evil into the world, or ruthlessly murder thousands of innocent people, as found in the Old Testament. When one reads the Old Testament with a critical eye, it becomes abundantly clear that this is not an all-loving, com-passionate God.

When Jesus referred to God the Father in the New Testament, he was not refer-ring to Yahweh. He was referring to the God above god — the True Father. Yahweh, according to the Gnostics, was an inferior angel and renegade god who broke away from the spiritual realm to play God here.

We have become trapped here with him, and must work to retrieve our divine spark, to nurture and to know it, so when we leave here we can find our way back home. Yaldabaoth (Yahweh), along with his dark helpers, the archons, keep mankind imprisoned within their material existence. They have barred the path of the soul from trying to ascend to our true spirit home after death. If we do not understand our spiritual condition, then there will be nothing we can do to improve it. Our home is not here. We are currently part of an alien world. We are spirit trapped in matter and must find our way out. We don't belong here on this Earth. We continue to reincarnate (stuck on the wheel, according to Buddhists) and are forced to return until we learn who we are and why we are here. Those who achieve gnosis no longer remain Christians or Buddhists, but become Christs, or Buddhas — enlightened souls who can choose to escape the trap.

The belief that the world is essentially evil falls under heavy criticism by many who claim this view is too negative. Negative or not, it may actually be true. And if true, that does not make Gnosticism a negative religion. There is goodness if we know where to look. We have addressed some of the positive aspects of gnosis on previous pages, especially on the divine spark and how it works within us and in the world. We have been thrown down into such a low material vibration that the divine spark fails to resonate strongly. Therefore, we do not recognize it. If we recognize it and get in touch with it, we can overcome our trapped spiritual condition, and receive a "triumph of the spirit."

This is what the early Gnostics taught. This is what was stamped out by Church authorities.

The Nag Hammadi Library

In about the year C.E. 367, hundreds of monks in Egypt challenged the Church's authority by engaging themselves in strict forms of self-discipline, and attempting spiritual insight through visions, solitude, and ecstatic experience. Athanasius, the powerful Archbishop of Alexandria, sent out an order to expel heretics from monasteries and eliminate all "apocryphal books" which contained anything that could be construed as heresy. The books Athanasius were after supported these monks in their independent search for truth. A Gnostic Christian community in Nag Hammadi, upper Egypt, became fearful of being charged with heresy, so priests gathered together their library of at least 52 books and sealed them in a large clay jar. They buried this jar in the sand beneath a cliff near their monastery. We believe this monastery to have been St. Pachomius, once located within sight of the cliff where the documents were discovered nearly 1600 years later. In 1945, two years before the discovery of the Dead Sea Scrolls, these books were unearthed by two peasants digging for fertilizer near the river Nile at Nag Hammadi.

The man who made the find was Muhammad Ali al-Samman. What he uncovered was a meter high, red earthenware jar. At first he was afraid to open it, thinking there might be a jinn, or evil spirit, inside. But after he considered the possibility of gold or treasure he and his brother opened it and found a number of papyrus books bound in leather. They brought the books home and put them in the straw near the oven. Their mother burned some of the discovered pages as fuel, but 1153 pages out of the original 1257 were still salvaged. These pages composed a total of 13 primitive, leather-bound volumes, containing the 52 smaller books, or tracates. After Muhammad became involved in a murder, he gave the books to the local priest. Once the local peasants figured out what they had, they divided the codices among themselves and sold them to middlemen for whatever price they could negotiate. These books were written in Coptic dialect, but many are unmistakable translations of Greek originals that date back to the second and third centuries C.E. They are the world's oldest known form of codex — a method of bookbinding which used stitching to secure the pages into leather bindings. To this day, no leather bound books are older.

The Director of the Coptic Museum, Togo Mina, was lucky enough to spot one of the books and purchased it from a dealer in 1946. He did not know at the time that there were others, but later teamed up with the Director-General of Egyptian Antiquities and Jean Doresse (*The Secret Books of the Egyptian Gnostics*) and proceeded to track most of them by 1949. It still took more than 32 years from their discovery for the books to become published in our more modern style in English — due to a combination of squabbling and general indifference among politicians, scholars, and antiquities dealers. These documents, valuable as they were, brought out the worst in people. Ownership was the big question and it did not get decided for years. We had crooked antique dealers, thieves, liars, a one-eyed bandit, and a respectable university professor who disguised himself and became a smuggler! At last, Professor James Robinson was able to have the books translated and then published in 1978.

Previous to this, the only written information we had on the Gnostics had been provided by their main opponents. Now we can know, and do know, what the Gnostics were all about. The Nag Hammadi library is unquestionably a heretical collection. It seems the monks who wrote them were Gnostic Christians who had not yet been run out of their monasteries.

One of the books, *The Gospel of Thomas,* contains 114 sayings attributed to Jesus and is considered by a large majority of scholars to be the most accurate collection of authentic sayings. And they predate the writing of New Testament gospels. We know this because some of the sayings from *Thomas* appear in the Bible, but without retaining the more original form found in *Thomas*. It's an absolute shame that this book continues to be suppressed by the Christian Church. Shame on them! We, as aware people, must recognize it for ourselves and make others aware. This is beginning to happen. Even the 1999 movie, "Stigmata", was inspired by this travesty. I went to Egypt, on a pilgrimage of sorts, to the Coptic Museum in Cairo, having heard that the original Nag Hammadi documents were stored there. One of the resulting photos appears above. The *Secret Book of John* ends at the top of the left hand page, followed by the beginning of the *Gospel According to Thomas*. A primary reason the book remains unrecognized, as mentioned earlier, is that it is attributed to Didymus Judas Thomas, the "twin" of Jesus. This is unacceptable to the Church. Yet *The Gospel of Thomas* was first written in Syria, as best as we can tell, and Thomas was widely known by the Syrian Church as being the brother of Jesus and founder of the Eastern churches, particularly Edessa.

It would only make sense that the brother of Jesus would have done his best to preserve his brother's sayings and teachings, and would have been present to hear most of them. One of my personal favorites is the following.

> If you bring forth what is within you, what you bring forth will save you. If you do not bring forth what is within you, what you do not bring forth will destroy you.
>
> —Jesus, *The Gospel of Thomas*

Jesus has said something here in direct opposition to a church that requires dependent followers — that we contain entirely *within ourselves* the potential for liberation or destruction.

Jesus had also said in Luke 17:21 that "the kingdom of God is within you." But to this day, the Church and most of its followers are waiting for the kingdom of God to come to *them*, to manifest as a physical event in history, rather than as a spiritual transformation. People want it done *for* them — the average person does not want to expend any energy toward their own salvation or enlightenment.

Jesus' own disciples made the same mistake and persisted in questioning him about the kingdom of God.

It will not come by waiting for it. It will not be a matter of saying "Here it is" or "There it is." Rather, the Kingdom of the Father is spread out upon the earth, and men do not see it.

—Jesus, *The Gospel of Thomas*

What men, who are spread out over the earth, do not see is the "divine spark" within them, which makes us all a part of the Kingdom. The Kingdom of God comes to those who access the divine spark and become "enlightened" by it. The world will not change, but our consciousness will. An internal transformation brings the Kingdom and, as Jesus tried to explain, it will not happen through any outer events in history. Perhaps the reason why we have yet to physically find God or had his material Kingdom arrive here is because collectively we *are* God, or are at least part of Him.

The possibility exists that our collective unconscious is God (or a part thereof). In the following definition of the collective unconscious, couldn't he also be talking about "God"? It was not written in that context, but it is something worth considering.

If it were possible to personify the unconscious, we might think of it as a collective human being combining the characteristics of both sexes, transcending youth and age, birth and death, and, from having at its command a human experience of one or two million years, practically immortal. If such a being existed, it would be exalted above all temporal change; the present would mean neither more nor less to it than any year in the hundredth millennium before Christ; it would be a dreamer of age-old dreams and, owing to its immeasurable experience, an incomparable prognosticator. It would have lived countless times over again the life of the individual, the family, the tribe, and the nation, and it would possess a living sense of the rhythm of growth, flowering, and decay.

—Carl Jung, *The Structure and Dynamics of the Psyche*

The Kingdom of God is not a physical place somewhere. Jesus said that if certain leaders told you that the Kingdom was in the sky, then the birds would get there before you would. It was a nice way of saying, "it's not physically real and you will never get there." He followed this by saying that the Kingdom is within. Somehow, our institutions would have us believe otherwise — contrary to Jesus' teachings. Based on his teachings, the idea that God's Kingdom will *physically* come to earth and reign for a thousand years is clearly suspect.

The shortest saying in *The Gospel of Thomas* is

Jesus said: Become passers by.

It is meant to be thought about. What does it mean? Gnostic Bishop Dr. Stephan Hoeller points out an Islamic saying in relation to this one:

The world is a bridge; pass over it, don't build on it.

We need to understand that this world is not our home. We come from the spirit, and are simply traveling through. So become passers by. This is a great lesson for non-attachment, stressed so often in Eastern religions. Stop being as possessive and engaged in planning things like you'll be here "forever," because you won't. Everything in this life is transient. Attaching oneself to transient things is futile.

The *Nag Hammadi Library* contains many fascinating books which offer further insights into early Christianity and the spiritual quest. *The Wisdom of Jesus Christ* contains a conversation between the resurrected Christ and his disciples. Mythological interpretations of *Genesis* include the *Paraphrase of Shem* and *The Apocalypse of Adam*. Other interesting tracts include The *Nature of the Rulers, On the Origin of the World, The Gospel of Truth,* and *The Gospel of the Egyptians*. All can be found within the larger volume, published as *The Nag Hammadi Library*.

Throughout history, some Gnostic groups have accepted the *Gospel of John* from the Bible in addition to these Nag Hammadi texts. After the four gospels were canonized, the *Gospel of John* was ignored in Rome for many decades. The Synoptic Gospels — of Matthew, Mark, and Luke — are considered separate from John (the word synoptic comes from synopsis). Irenaeus detailed much opposition to the Fourth Gospel, but those who refused it were not charged with heresy if they accepted the other three. The Gnostics who accepted only John from the canon were, of course, considered heretics.

If one compares the *Gospel of Truth* from Nag Hammadi with John, strong parallels are found between them — but with the more solid Gnostic ideas missing from John. Although some Gnostic ideas remained in John, its writer repudiates Gnosticism's basic convictions. That is how and why John made it into the canon. The verb "to know" was used 133 times, but the noun "knowledge" (*gnosis*) was never used. He used the verb "to believe" 95 times, but the noun "belief," or "faith" (*pistis*) was never used. *Gnosis* and *pistis* were key Gnostic words at the time, and their exclusion is not the result of mere chance.

Setting Gnosis Apart

A major point made clear from these writings is that Gnosticism was not so much a Christian or Jewish off-shoot, but a religion all to its own. It surfaced within the various religious systems of antiquity, expressed its otherworldly message while borrowing from other faiths, and fused it all into a spiritual religion. Although it is unclear beyond this as to exactly how Gnosticism developed, most scholars agree that it was, in fact, a separate religion.

Gnosticism never officially organized itself because that is precisely what it was fighting against — becoming dogmatized and simplified for consumption to the masses. At the same time, this was its downfall. By not organizing enough to protect itself, the movement left itself open to vicious persecutions and violent reactions by groups less spiritually advanced. Gnosticism by itself, in the past as well as today, does not lend itself well to mass religion.

Your own truth and your own spiritual advancement is done best on an individual basis. If you find this book interesting then you might want to continue with the exercises in the Appendix and devote yourself to your SELF. Feel free to go beyond the scope of this book and continue forward with focus and intensity, into the inner realm of truth. Take it as a challenge to make the effort and look. A real triumph of the spirit could await you.

Remember, the Church fathers were interested in creating a religion which anyone could follow easily, not a religion for a select group of spiritual seekers or intellectuals. They chopped out many deeper truths in order to feed the masses a homogenized version of religion. It is up to you to find those deeper truths.

This chapter was an excerpt from Paul Tice's larger work entitled, Triumph of the Human Spirit: The Greatest Achievements of the Human Soul and How Its Power can Change Your Life, *(ISBN 1-885395-57-4) available from The Book Tree at 1-800-700-8733 or can be ordered from your favorite bookseller.*

INDEX

Triumph of the Human Spirit: The Greatest Achievements of the Human Soul and How Its Power Can Change Your Life, **by Paul Tice.** A triumph of the human spirit happens when we know we are right

about something, put our heart into achieving its goal, and then succeed. There is no better feeling. People throughout history have triumphed while fighting for the highest ideal of all -- spiritual truth. Tice brings you back to relive and explore history's most incredible spiritual moments, bringing you into the lives of visionaries and great leaders who were in touch with their souls and followed their hearts. They explored God in their own way, exposed corruption and false teachings, or freed themselves and others from suppression. People like Gandhi, Joan of Arc, and Dr. King expressed exactly what they believed and changed the entire course of history. They were eliminated through violence, but on a spiritual level achieved victory because of their strong moral cause. Their spirit lives on, and the world was greatly improved. Tice covers other movements and people who may have physically failed, but spiritually triumphed. This book not only documents the history of spiritual giants, it shows how you can achieve your own spiritual triumph. In today's world we are free to explore the truth without fear of being tortured or executed. As a result, the rewards are great. Various exercises will strengthen the soul and reveal its hidden power. One can discover their true spiritual source with this work and will be able to tap into it. This is the perfect book for all those who believe in spiritual freedom and have a passion for the truth. **ISBN 1-885395-57-4 · 295 pages · 6 x 9 · trade paper · illustrated · $19.95**

Mysteries Explored: The Search for Human Origins, UFOs, and Religious Beginnings, **by Jack Barranger and Paul Tice.** Jack Barranger and Paul Tice are two authors who have combined forces in an overall investigation into human origins, religion, mythology, UFOs, and other unexplained phenomena. In the first chapter, "The Legacy of Zecharia Sitchin", Barranger covers the importance of Sitchin's *Earth Chronicles* books, which is creating a revolution in the way we look at our past. In "The First Dragon" chapter, Tice examines the earliest known story containing dragons, coming from Sumerian/Babylonian mythology. In "Past Shock", Barranger suggests that events which happened thousands of years ago very strongly impact humanity today. In "UFOs: From Earth or Outer Space?" Tice explores the evidence for aliens being from other earthly dimensions as opposed to having an extraterrestrial origin. "Is Religion Harmful?" looks at the origins of religion and why the entire idea may no longer be working for us, while "A Call to Heresy" shows how Jesus and the Buddha were considered heretics in their day, and how we have reached a critical point in our present spiritual development that requires another such leap. Aside from these chapters, the book also contains a number of outrageous (but discontinued) newsletters, including: Promethean Fire, Pleiadian Poop, and Intrusions. **ISBN 1-58509-101-4 · 104 pages · 6 x 9 · trade paper · $12.95**

Jumpin' Jehovah: Exposing the Atrocities of the Old Testament God, **by Paul Tice.** Was Jehovah a criminal? Was he psychotic? In the

realm of the gods, was Jehovah just a renegade punk gone wild? Paul Tice has collected all the dirt on this shady historical character. Once you read this book, your views on God will never be the same again. Jehovah is stripped bare of all his fabricated "godliness" and we discover in this book an entity with no sense of ethics, forgiveness or compassion. Jehovah delighted in roasting people alive and tormenting his followers in a variety of creative ways. Tice takes us from the very beginning, when this crafty character first came on the scene, and shows us how he conned and bullied his way to the top of the godly heap. Jehovah then maintained his standing through threats and coercion— and when that didn't work, he did what any mentally deranged god would do: he just moved in and killed people. Basic theological questions are explored like: Was Jehovah really a god, or a demon? Why did Jehovah never promise a heaven or any kind of reward to his followers? Does any entity who murders thousands of devoted followers deserve to be worshipped? What are the differences between a false god and a true one? Jehovah has stopped punishing people in terrible ways, so it's probably safe to buy this book. **ISBN 1-58509-102-2 · 104 pages · 6 x 9 · trade paper · $12.95**

122

Of Heaven and Earth: Essays Presented at the First Sitchin Studies Day, edited by Zecharia Sitchin. ISBN 1-885395-17-5 • 164 pages • 5 1/2 x 8 1/2 • trade paper • illustrated • $14.95

God Games: What Do You Do Forever?, by Neil Freer. ISBN 1-885395-39-6 • 312 pages • 6 x 9 • trade paper • $19.95

Space Travelers and the Genesis of the Human Form: Evidence of Intelligent Contact in the Solar System, by Joan d'Arc. ISBN 1-58509-127-8 • 208 pages • 6 x 9 • trade paper • illustrated • $18.95

Humanity's Extraterrestrial Origins: ET Influences on Humankind's Biological and Cultural Evolution, by Dr. Arthur David Horn with Lynette Mallory-Horn. ISBN 3-931652-31-9 • 373 pages • 6 x 9 • trade paper • $17.00

Past Shock: The Origin of Religion and Its Impact on the Human Soul, by Jack Barranger. ISBN 1-885395-08-6 • 126 pages • 6 x 9 • trade paper • illustrated • $12.95

Flying Serpents and Dragons: The Story of Mankind's Reptilian Past, by R.A. Boulay. ISBN 1-885395-38-8 • 276 pages • 6 x 9 • trade paper • illustrated • $19.95

Triumph of the Human Spirit: The Greatest Achievements of the Human Soul and How Its Power Can Change Your Life by Paul Tice. ISBN 1-885395-57-4 • 295 pages • 6 x 9 • trade paper • illustrated • $19.95

Mysteries Explored: The Search for Human Origins, UFOs, and Religious Beginnings, by Jack Barranger and Paul Tice. ISBN 1-58509-101-4 • 104 pages • 6 x 9 • trade paper • $12.95

Mushrooms and Mankind: The Impact of Mushrooms on Human Consciousness and Religion, by James Arthur. ISBN 1-58509-151-0 • 180 pages • 6 x 9 • trade paper • $16.95

Vril or Vital Magnetism, with an Introduction by Paul Tice.ISBN 1-58509-030-1 • 124 pages • 5 1/2 x 8 1/2 • trade paper • $12.95

The Odic Force: Letters on Od and Magnetism, by Karl von Reichenbach. ISBN 1-58509-001-8 • 192 pages • 6 x 9 • trade paper • $15.95

The New Revelation: The Coming of a New Spiritual Paradigm, by Arthur Conan Doyle.ISBN 1-58509-220-7 • 124 pages • 6 x 9 • trade paper • $12.95

The Astral World: Its Scenes, Dwellers, and Phenomena, by Swami Panchadasi. ISBN 1-58509-071-9 • 104 pages • 6 x 9 • trade paper • $11.95

Reason and Belief: The Impact of Scientific Discovery on Religious and Spiritual Faith, by Sir Oliver Lodge. ISBN 1-58509-226-6 • 180 pages • 6 x 9 • trade paper • $17.95

William Blake: A Biography, by Basil De Selincourt. ISBN 1-58509-225-8 • 384 pages • 6 x 9 • trade paper • $28.95

The Divine Pymander: And Other Writings of Hermes Trismegistus, translated by John D. Chambers. ISBN 1-58509-046-8 • 196 pages • 6 x 9 • trade paper • $16.95

Theosophy and The Secret Doctrine, by Harriet L. Henderson. Includes *H.P. Blavatsky: An Outline of Her Life,* by Herbert Whyte, ISBN 1-58509-075-1 • 132 pages • 6 x 9 • trade paper • $13.95

The Light of Egypt, Volume One: The Science of the Soul and the Stars, by Thomas H. Burgoyne. ISBN 1-58509-051-4 • 320 pages • 6 x 9 • trade paper • illustrated • $24.95

The Light of Egypt, Volume Two: The Science of the Soul and the Stars, by Thomas H. Burgoyne. ISBN 1-58509-052-2 • 224 pages • 6 x 9 • trade paper • illustrated • $17.95

The Jumping Frog and 18 Other Stories: 19 Unforgettable Mark Twain Stories, by Mark Twain. ISBN 1-58509-200-2 • 128 pages • 6 x 9 • trade paper • $12.95

The Devil's Dictionary: A Guidebook for Cynics, by Ambrose Bierce. ISBN 1-58509-016-6 • 144 pages • 6 x 9 • trade paper • $12.95

The Smoky God: Or The Voyage to the Inner World, by Willis George Emerson. ISBN 1-58509-067-0 • 184 pages • 6 x 9 • trade paper • illustrated • $15.95

A Short History of the World, by H.G. Wells.ISBN 1-58509-211-8 • 320 pages • 6 x 9 • trade paper • $24.95

The Voyages and Discoveries of the Companions of Columbus, by Washington Irving.ISBN 1-58509-500-1 • 352 pages • 6 x 9 • hard cover • $39.95

History of Baalbek, by Michel Alouf. ISBN 1-58509-063-8 • 196 pages • 5 x 8 • trade paper • illustrated • $15.95

Ancient Egyptian Masonry: The Building Craft, by Sommers Clarke and R. Engelback. ISBN 1-58509-059-X • 350 pages • 6 x 9 • trade paper • illustrated • $26.95

That Old Time Religion: The Story of Religious Foundations, by Jordan Maxwell and Paul Tice. ISBN 1-58509-100-6 • 220 pages • 6 x 9 • trade paper • $19.95

Jumpin' Jehovah: Exposing the Atrocities of the Old Testament God, by Paul Tice. ISBN 1-58509-102-2 • 104 pages • 6 x 9 • trade paper • $12.95

The Book of Enoch: A Work of Visionary Revelation and Prophecy, Revealing Divine Secrets and Fantastic Information about Creation, Salvation, Heaven and Hell, translated by R. H. Charles. ISBN 1-58509-019-0 • 152 pages • 5 1/2 x 8 1/2 • trade paper • $13.95

The Book of Enoch: Translated from the Editor's Ethiopic Text and Edited with an Enlarged Introduction, Notes and Indexes, Together with a Reprint of the Greek Fragments, edited by R. H. Charles. ISBN 1-58509-080-8 • 448 pages • 6 x 9 • trade paper • $34.95

The Book of the Secrets of Enoch, translated from the Slavonic by W. R. Morfill. Edited, with Introduction and Notes by R. H. Charles. ISBN 1-58509-020-4 • 148 pages • 5 1/2 x 8 1/2 • trade paper • $13.95

Enuma Elish: The Seven Tablets of Creation, Volume One, by L. W. King. ISBN 1-58509-041-7 • 236 pages • 6 x 9 • trade paper • illustrated • $18.95

Enuma Elish: The Seven Tablets of Creation, Volume Two, by L. W. King. ISBN 1-58509-042-5 • 260 pages • 6 x 9 • trade paper • illustrated • $19.95

Enuma Elish, Volumes One and Two: The Seven Tablets of Creation, by L. W. King. Two volumes from above bound as one. ISBN 1-58509-043-3 • 496 pages • 6 x 9 • trade paper • illustrated • $38.90

The Archko Volume: Documents that Claim Proof to the Life, Death, and Resurrection of Christ, by Drs. McIntosh and Twyman. ISBN 1-58509-082-4 • 248 pages • 6 x 9 • trade paper • $20.95

The Lost Language of Symbolism: An Inquiry into the Origin of Certain Letters, Words, Names, Fairy-Tales, Folklore, and Mythologies, by Harold Bayley. ISBN 1-58509-070-0 • 384 pages • 6 x 9 • trade paper • $27.95

The Book of Jasher: A Suppressed Book that was Removed from the Bible, Referred to in Joshua and Second Samuel, translated by Albinus Alcuin (800 AD). ISBN 1-58509-081-6 • 304 pages • 6 x 9 • trade paper • $24.95

The Bible's Most Embarrassing Moments, with an Introduction by Paul Tice. ISBN 1-58509-025-5 • 172 pages • 5 x 8 • trade paper • $14.95

History of the Cross: The Pagan Origin and Idolatrous Adoption and Worship of the Image, by Henry Dana Ward. ISBN 1-58509-056-5 • 104 pages • 6 x 9 • trade paper • illustrated • $11.95

Was Jesus Influenced by Buddhism? A Comparative Study of the Lives and Thoughts of Gautama and Jesus, by Dwight Goddard. ISBN 1-58509-027-1 • 252 pages • 6 x 9 • trade paper • $19.95

History of the Christian Religion to the Year Two Hundred, by Charles B. Waite. ISBN 1-885395-15-9 • 556 pages. • 6 x 9 • hard cover • $25.00

Symbols, Sex, and the Stars, by Ernest Busenbark. ISBN 1-885395-19-1 • 396 pages • 5 1/2 x 8 1/2 • trade paper • $22.95

History of the First Council of Nice: A World's Christian Convention, A.D. 325, by Dean Dudley. ISBN 1-58509-023-9 • 132 pages • 5 1/2 x 8 1/2 • trade paper • $12.95

The World's Sixteen Crucified Saviors, by Kersey Graves. ISBN 1-58509-018-2 • 436 pages • 5 1/2 x 8 1/2 • trade paper • $29.95

Babylonian Influence on the Bible and Popular Beliefs: A Comparative Study of Genesis I.2, by A. Smythe Palmer. ISBN 1-58509-000-X • 124 pages • 6 x 9 • trade paper • $12.95

Biography of Satan: Exposing the Origins of the Devil, by Kersey Graves. ISBN 1-885395-11-6 • 168 pages • 5 1/2 x 8 1/2 • trade paper • $13.95

The Malleus Maleficarum: The Notorious Handbook Once Used to Condemn and Punish "Witches", by Heinrich Kramer and James Sprenger. ISBN 1-58509-098-0 • 332 pages • 6 x 9 • trade paper • $25.95

Crux Ansata: An Indictment of the Roman Catholic Church, by H. G. Wells. ISBN 1-58509-210-X • 160 pages • 6 x 9 • trade paper • $14.95

Emanuel Swedenborg: The Spiritual Columbus, by U.S.E. (William Spear). ISBN 1-58509-096-4 • 208 pages • 6 x 9 • trade paper • $17.95

Dragons and Dragon Lore, by Ernest Ingersoll. ISBN 1-58509-021-2 • 228 pages • 6 x 9 • trade paper • illustrated • $17.95

The Vision of God, by Nicholas of Cusa. ISBN 1-58509-004-2 • 160 pages • 5 x 8 • trade paper • $13.95

The Historical Jesus and the Mythical Christ: Separating Fact From Fiction, by Gerald Massey. ISBN 1-58509-073-5 • 244 pages • 6 x 9 • trade paper • $18.95

Gog and Magog: The Giants in Guildhall; Their Real and Legendary History, with an Account of Other Giants at Home and Abroad, by F.W. Fairholt. ISBN 1-58509-084-0 • 172 pages • 6 x 9 • trade paper • $16.95

The Origin and Evolution of Religion, by Albert Churchward. ISBN 1-58509-078-6 • 504 pages • 6 x 9 • trade paper • $39.95

The Origin of Biblical Traditions, by Albert T. Clay. ISBN 1-58509-065-4 • 220 pages • 5 1/2 x 8 1/2 • trade paper • $17.95

Aryan Sun Myths, by Sarah Elizabeth Titcomb, Introduction by Charles Morris. ISBN 1-58509-069-7 • 192 pages • 6 x 9 • trade paper • $15.95

The Social Record of Christianity, by Joseph McCabe. Includes *The Lies and Fallacies of the Encyclopedia Britannica,* ISBN 1-58509-215-0 • 204 pages • 6 x 9 • trade paper • $17.95

The History of the Christian Religion and Church During the First Three Centuries, by Dr. Augustus Neander. ISBN 1-58509-077-8 • 112 pages • 6 x 9 • trade paper • $12.95

Ancient Symbol Worship: Influence of the Phallic Idea in the Religions of Antiquity, by Hodder M. Westropp and C. Staniland Wake. ISBN 1-58509-048-4 • 120 pages • 6 x 9 • trade paper • illustrated • $12.95

The Gnosis: Or Ancient Wisdom in the Christian Scriptures, by William Kingsland. ISBN 1-58509-047-6 • 232 pages • 6 x 9 • trade paper • $18.95

The Evolution of the Idea of God: An Inquiry into the Origin of Religions, by Grant Allen. ISBN 1-58509-074-3 • 160 pages • 6 x 9 • trade paper • $14.95

Sun Lore of All Ages: A Survey of Solar Mythology, Folklore, Customs, Worship, Festivals, and Superstition, by William Tyler Olcott. ISBN 1-58509-044-1 • 316 pages • 6 x 9 • trade paper • $24.95

Nature Worship: An Account of Phallic Faiths and Practices Ancient and Modern, by the Author of Phallicism with an Introduction by Tedd St. Rain. ISBN 1-58509-049-2 • 112 pages • 6 x 9 • trade paper • illustrated • $12.95

Life and Religion, by Max Muller. ISBN 1-885395-10-8 • 237 pages • 5 1/2 x 8 1/2 • trade paper • $14.95

Jesus: God, Man, or Myth? An Examination of the Evidence, by Herbert Cutner. ISBN 1-58509-072-7 • 304 pages • 6 x 9 • trade paper • $23.95

Pagan and Christian Creeds: Their Origin and Meaning, by Edward Carpenter. ISBN 1-58509-024-7 • 316 pages • 5 1/2 x 8 1/2 • trade paper • $24.95

The Christ Myth: A Study, by Elizabeth Evans. ISBN 1-58509-037-9 • 136 pages • 6 x 9 • trade paper • $13.95

Popery: Foe of the Church and the Republic, by Joseph F. Van Dyke. ISBN 1-58509-058-1 • 336 pages • 6 x 9 • trade paper • illustrated • $25.95

Career of Religious Ideas, by Hudson Tuttle. ISBN 1-58509-066-2 • 172 pages • 5 x 8 • trade paper • $15.95

Buddhist Suttas: Major Scriptural Writings from Early Buddhism, by T.W. Rhys Davids. ISBN 1-58509-079-4 • 376 pages • 6 x 9 • trade paper • $27.95

Early Buddhism, by T. W. Rhys Davids. Includes *Buddhist Ethics: The Way to Salvation?,* by Paul Tice. ISBN 1-58509-076-X • 112 pages • 6 x 9 • trade paper • $12.95

The Fountain-Head of Religion: A Comparative Study of the Principal Religions of the World and a Manifestation of their Common Origin from the Vedas, by Ganga Prasad. ISBN 1-58509-054-9 • 276 pages • 6 x 9 • trade paper • $22.95

India: What Can It Teach Us?, by Max Muller. ISBN 1-58509-064-6 • 284 pages • 5 1/2 x 8 1/2 • trade paper • $22.95

Matrix of Power: How the World has Been Controlled by Powerful People Without Your Knowledge, by Jordan Maxwell. ISBN 1-58509-120-0 • 104 pages • 6 x 9 • trade paper • $12.95

Cyberculture Counterconspiracy: A Steamshovel Web Reader, Volume One, edited by Kenn Thomas. ISBN 1-58509-125-1 • 180 pages • 6 x 9 • trade paper • illustrated • $16.95

Cyberculture Counterconspiracy: A Steamshovel Web Reader, Volume Two, edited by Kenn Thomas. ISBN 1-58509-126-X • 132 pages • 6 x 9 • trade paper • illustrated • $13.95

Oklahoma City Bombing: The Suppressed Truth, by Jon Rappoport. ISBN 1-885395-22-1 • 112 pages • 5 1/2 x 8 1/2 • trade paper • $12.95

The Protocols of the Learned Elders of Zion, by Victor Marsden. ISBN 1-58509-015-8 • 312 pages • 6 x 9 • trade paper • $24.95

Secret Societies and Subversive Movements, by Nesta H. Webster. ISBN 1-58509-092-1 • 432 pages • 6 x 9 • trade paper • $29.95

The Secret Doctrine of the Rosicrucians, by Magus Incognito. ISBN 1-58509-091-3 • 256 pages • 6 x 9 • trade paper • $20.95

The Origin and Evolution of Freemasonry: Connected with the Origin and Evolution of the Human Race, by Albert Churchward. ISBN 1-58509-029-8 • 240 pages • 6 x 9 • trade paper • $18.95

The Lost Key: An Explanation and Application of Masonic Symbols, by Prentiss Tucker. ISBN 1-58509-050-6 • 192 pages • 6 x 9 • trade paper • illustrated • $15.95

The Character, Claims, and Practical Workings of Freemasonry, by Rev. C.G. Finney. ISBN 1-58509-094-8 • 288 pages • 6 x 9 • trade paper • $22.95

The Secret World Government or "The Hidden Hand": The Unrevealed in History, by Maj.-Gen., Count Cherep-Spiridovich. ISBN 1-58509-093-X • 270 pages • 6 x 9 • trade paper • $21.95

The Magus, Book One: A Complete System of Occult Philosophy, by Francis Barrett. ISBN 1-58509-031-X • 200 pages • 6 x 9 • trade paper • illustrated • $16.95

The Magus, Book Two: A Complete System of Occult Philosophy, by Francis Barrett. ISBN 1-58509-032-8 • 220 pages • 6 x 9 • trade paper • illustrated • $17.95

The Magus, Book One and Two: A Complete System of Occult Philosophy, by Francis Barrett. ISBN 1-58509-033-6 • 420 pages • 6 x 9 • trade paper • illustrated • $34.90

The Key of Solomon The King, by S. Liddell MacGregor Mathers. ISBN 1-58509-022-0 • 152 pages • 6 x 9 • trade paper • illustrated • $12.95

Magic and Mystery in Tibet, by Alexandra David-Neel. ISBN 1-58509-097-2 • 352 pages • 6 x 9 • trade paper • $26.95

The Comte de St. Germain, by I. Cooper Oakley. ISBN 1-58509-068-9 • 280 pages • 6 x 9 • trade paper • illustrated • $22.95

Alchemy Rediscovered and Restored, by A. Cockren. ISBN 1-58509-028-X • 156 pages • 5 1/2 x 8 1/2 • trade paper • $13.95

The 6th and 7th Books of Moses, with an Introduction by Paul Tice. ISBN 1-58509-045-X • 188 pages • 6 x 9 • trade paper • illustrated • $16.95

Printed in the United States
131358LV00007BA/208/A

9 781585 091003